FWD March

Brady, wishing you all the best as you continue to share your talents with the world. Happy reading!

Evan Chandler

FWD March
Living in a World of Music and Motion

George Scott Chandler

Copyright © 2015 by George Scott Chandler
All rights reserved.
First Printing, 2015
ISBN: 1511960337
ISBN 13: 9781511960335
Library of Congress Catalog Number: 2015907215
CreateSpace Independent Publishing Platform
North Charleston, South Carolina

FRONT COVER PHOTO Blue Devils courtesy of Hans Kloppert
BACK COVER PHOTO courtesy of Jen Lowe
Blue Devils PHOTOS courtesy of Blue Devils
(photographers Hans Kloppert, Erik J Skinner, Jennifer Lowe)
Spirit of Atlanta PHOTO courtesy of Mike Morris
Spirit of Atlanta with Tam Easterwood PHOTO courtesy of Ken Diggs
WGI PHOTOS courtesy of Winter Guard International (photographer Sue Johnson)
Blue Devils
4065 Nelson Ave
Concord, CA 94520
www.Bluedevils.org

For my father
Clifford Sanders Chandler, Jr.

Acknowledgements

It would be impossible for me to proceed without offering my heartfelt thanks to the late, great A. R. Casavant. Often known as the father of precision marching, A.R Casavant could very well be the most influential person ever on our marching universe. A true pioneer, innovator and yes, choreographer, his concepts and techniques have been practiced and studied in the United States and around the world. We owe so much to his vision and his artistry.

Thank You to Mark Metzger for standing by my side for twenty plus years.

Thank You Jay, Shirlee, Karl, Dave, Jeff and Ron for letting me share this with you and for giving me encouragement.

Thanks to the late Fred J. Miller who was a marching arts giant in his own right. To Marlene, the entire Miller family, and everyone at FJM, Inc. thank you for allowing me and countless others to make dreams a reality.

Table of Contents

Acknowledgements ix
Preface xiii
Introduction xix
1 Little Boy Who? 1
2 You Dream (a Lot) 19
3 Momentum 27
4 Experience 36
5 Blessings in Disguise 44
6 Live/Play/Live 54
7 Applause, A-pause 65
8 Compete 76
9 Friend/Foe 87
10 Judge 95
11 The Spinning Compass 105
12 Inevitable 116
13 Ideas 128
14 *Felliniesque* 139
15 Desire Overcomes Doubt 155
16 There's Something to Be Said for... 161
17 Cornbread Dressing 174
18 Putting It Together (Well, for Now) 181
19 Dear Performers... 202
20 Pull It in 207
    About the Author 210
    Author's Notes 212
    Glossary 214

Preface

Foreword (March)

I wanted to write something about the worlds of color guard, drum and bugle corps, and marching bands. It's the world I exist in and it's inhabited by some of the most talented, creative, and dedicated people you will ever meet. It's a universe that can often go unnoticed, but has existed for as long as pageantry has served global cultures. Even if you are not familiar with its existence you might be surprised at how it has permeated your life. It is music. It is rhythm. It is motion. It is color. It is marching. It has evolved just as any art advances. Born out of function and transformed into artistic expression, it's an enigmatic wonder. There are performers who will astound your senses with expertise, communication, and skill. They move it forward.

As I began to jot down my various ideas I began to realize that I was telling the story of my personal arrival into this exceptional world. We pour our lives into who and what we are, and I could not separate who I am personally from who I am professionally. There's something ironic about the forward references when looking back. I'm aware of that fact. But looking at how you arrive somewhere doesn't ignore the constant desire to keep some crazy sort of progression forward. It's a life. And here's how I like to think that everything for me began.

The time is World War II and there are three young army servicemen stationed close to Greensboro, North Carolina. These three young soldiers are proud patriots and I imagine they carry themselves with all the swagger and style of the time. It's straight up *On The Town* and very Gene Kelly-esque with fast-paced conversations and bravado that makes them look like any second they could give birth to some cool, sly pirouette and pose. There's a slick car, lit cigarettes, and big band music in the air as they head to a local bowling alley. One of the young men has arranged for a meeting with three beautiful nursing students from a local hospital. It will be a photogenic night of Americana. The three young nurses know exactly how to detail themselves in the fashion of the era and are confident in the innocence and excitement of the night ahead. They are smart and stylish and know exactly how to forge a new era of women having a family and a career.

The six of them arrive at the bowling alley at pretty much the same time. Greetings and introductions are exchanged. The three perfect gentlemen and the three beautiful young nurses make their way to the door. The procession seems to pair them up by chance as they enter the establishment. The last couple through the doorway reintroduce themselves and shares that kind of cinematic glance that takes a pause to fully comprehend. The scene gradually gets swept away by the sound of bowling pins and conversations, spirited music, and oh yes, the unforgettable buzz of destiny.

Throughout the years, I used to make my mother and father tell that story over and over. I could picture it, paint it in my head and soak up the romance in every embellished nuance. That last couple through the doorway on that easiest of Carolina nights were my parents. My father was that young soldier and my mother the young nurse. And just by the happenstance of an unplanned place in line, they walked through that doorway into what would be more than fifty years of marriage. I am a result of that chance meeting all those years ago. It was a blind date that would last a lifetime.

I used to think a lot about who I might be if even one person had altered the simple order of those six people. *Would I be me? Would I have met the people I have known? Would I have heard the same music or danced the same steps? Would I be swimming in memories while I sit on the 34th floor of this Tokyo hotel on a rainy Sunday night?* Mostly I think I'm lucky that I knew those two starry eyed young people that would become my parents. And even when forward motion can carry you up and down, over and through, you can count on gratitude to shed a little light on the journey. Here we go, let's move forward.

If
By Rudyard Kipling

If you can keep your head when all about you
Are losing theirs and blaming it on you,
If you can trust yourself when all men doubt you,
But make allowance for their doubting too;
If you can wait and not be tired by waiting,
Or being lied about, don't deal in lies,
Or being hated, don't give way to hating,
And yet don't look too good, nor talk too wise:

If you can dream—and not make dreams your master;
If you can think—and not make thoughts your aim;
If you can meet with Triumph and Disaster
And treat those two impostors just the same;
If you can bear to hear the truth you've spoken
Twisted by knaves to make a trap for fools,
Or watch the things you gave your life to, broken,
And stoop and build 'em up with worn-out tools:

If you can make one heap of all your winnings
And risk it on one turn of pitch-and-toss,
And lose, and start again at your beginnings
And never breathe a word about your loss;
If you can force your heart and nerve and sinew
To serve your turn long after they are gone,
And so hold on when there is nothing in you
Except the Will which says to them: "Hold on!"

If you can talk with crowds and keep your virtue,
Or walk with Kings—nor lose the common touch,

If neither foes nor loving friends can hurt you,
If all men count with you, but none too much;
If you can fill the unforgiving minute
With sixty seconds' worth of distance run,
Yours is the Earth and everything that's in it,
And—which is more—you'll be a Man, my son.

('Brother Square-Toes'—*Rewards and Fairies*)

Introduction

Ron Nankervis and I sat on the lively set of the television series *Glee*. Ron is the CEO of Winter Guard International. WGI is the premier governing organization for Indoor Color Guard/Percussion competition and sponsors a multitude of contest and clinics for all levels of indoor Guards and drum lines. We watched from the makeshift set of an auditorium as details of the busy day of shooting unfolded before us. Eric Stoltz, an incredible actor/director, was guiding the day's process that included a group of WGI's talented performers spinning flags. More often than not when people who have never seen the colorful flags in motion or manipulated through space and tossed into the air, they are amazed. That amazement leads to curiosity and Eric Stoltz was no exception. His director's eye quickly assessed this incredibly visual amalgamation and how it would be shot amid the considerations of the song, the scene, and the story line of this particular episode. He approached Ron and I with another often heard query, "Where did this come from?" *OK Scott, it's Eric Stoltz! Choose your words wisely. How on earth do we explain this? You know he doesn't have time to sit down and listen to some lengthy rambling explanation.* We kept it simple as most people prefer. And I'll have to paraphrase because honestly I am sure that I babbled like an incoherent demented fan-droid. I sidestepped the global context in favor of a simplified explanation. I'm certainly no master of vexillology.

"Well, at first it was just a function of carrying the American flag. Then there were flags that were presented to add color. At some point, someone figured out they could move these flags and, more than that, move them to the music!"

I have no idea if it made any sense to him. He was gracious (and impeccably dressed I might add), and quickly returned to the task at hand.

It's true though, somewhere a long the line some incredibly creative soul figured out that flags added color to the marching band and had the ingenious discovery that these flags could be manipulated. It must have been enlightening and surprising to witness the first spin or side-slam of this archetypical instrument. In Europe you can watch as flag jugglers toss and exchange large swing flags dressed in 13th-century costume. Flags have long been used for spectacle, decoration, and illustration. Obviously the act of manipulating flags for the thrill of the onlooker came long before we thought of it in this country. The ceremonial use of flags and weapons has an indubitably long and significant lineage.

The American flag had people guarding it, too. Marching members who, complete with a sidearm—a sword, pistol, or rifle—were there to guard the national colors. The same thought must have occurred or, as I like to imagine, someone like me in a moment of boredom or the need to provide comic relief, began to spin the equipment they were carrying. Soldiers have long had a manual of arms and displayed a disciplined, regimented presentation of handling the rifle and saber. At some point, it became an instrument of motion, excitement, and musical interpretation. The act became multi-dimensional. In much the same way the drum major's baton, once only used for keeping time, changed, and evolved into a twirling instrument of athleticism and incredible skill.

It's not unusual that people are oblivious to the details of our existence. But I often say to my fellow enthusiast that there are plenty of unknown activities in the world. How many people really know the specifics of rhythmic gymnastics with their hoops, ribbons, balls, and clubs? It's amazing and yet often goes unnoticed in the universe of available sports events. There are so many art forms, talents, and skills that never venture into the mainstream awareness. There are practitioners of exceptional talents that never become rich or famous. In my younger days I struggled deeply with the fact that I was obsessed with something that so many people were unaware of and sometimes quite overt in their disdain. I felt the need to let everyone know what this odd, skillful, and quite artful activity was all about. People—and perhaps it's human nature—out of ignorance often ignite a negative response when it comes to things they don't readily know about. Not only has that ignorance and unwillingness to see things in another way impacted my career, but I also carry a deep-rooted sensitivity to how such closed-mindedness impacts the world at large.

If you travel often you probably have a routine. I certainly do. I have my time frame of travel to the airport, how long to delay passing through security until just the right moment for the boarding announcement, what magazine(s) to purchase, what snacks to have in the bag if needed, even the tiny tap on the outside of the airplane entrance for luck as I enter. And if you travel often enough you start to be prepared for any adjustments to the routine or surprise schedule changes or delays. You have a plan. I took my first flight when I was twelve years old and ever since then I've developed a pretty good sense of what to expect and how to pass the time. But throughout the years the one thing that has evolved and changed the most is my answer to the oft-heard fellow passenger's inquiry: "What is it that you do?"

The question comes in a multitude of forms and people are pleasant in their curiosity. I have come up with a long list of shadowy, indistinct answers that could sound as general as plain-packaged generic food. Until many years ago, I stumbled upon the easiest solution—simply tell the truth. Fortunately, I have found the truthful response to spark an honest interest from the inquisitive passenger and only on rare occasions has any kind of judgment seeped through the conversation. I think I always assumed the other person would not really understand or, for that matter, care, but I have found people to be genuinely interested. And people come to their own understanding through their own personal experience, which can make for fascinating insight into how the "outside" world defines what I do. They may not know color guard or drum corps, but they may know about drill or dance teams, the world famous Kilgore Rangerettes, cheerleading competitions on television, or the halftime production at a college bowl game.

My simple answer is usually this: "I work with marching bands, drum and bugle corps, color guards, and dancers." Now, depending upon the person, the conversation can veer into all kinds of directions. There is almost always some way that most people can relate.

Sometimes with a calculated inspiration, often blindly with a dose of naivety, I seem to march forward…one foot in front of the other. *Here we go.*

CHAPTER 1

Little Boy Who?

Rome, Georgia is not a huge city, but it's not a small town either. When I was growing up I was proud of our community and actually thought that it was a much larger place than it actually was, but most of all I was intrigued by its rich history and multi-cultural past. We weren't bound only by stereotypes and southern punch lines. We may not have been New York City, but we had more than one stoplight and didn't live next to moonshine stills. (That is, not that I was aware of.) And being in that mid-range size meant that our community wasn't foreign to social confusion. There were all kinds of people, a multitude of churches of varying religions and denominations, and a wealth of educational institutions. And I was growing up amid the tension of civil rights and an ever-changing landscape of what being "southern" meant.

I come from a long line of democrats. My parents, "Louise and C.S.," were deeply religious but progressive thinkers with what I like to call a healthy dose of caution. Their cautious attitude depended on the subject matter and it always depended on their understanding of the issue. Pretty standard stuff I'd say. They represented the epitome of the saying, "They did the best they knew how, and when they knew better they did better."

My mother, a registered nurse, had worked in several aspects of the medical field and eventually worked for years until retirement at Berry College. I adored my mother, thought she was beautiful, intelligent, and highly professional. She was kind, gentle, and quick to react with her knowledge of medical care. It's true. When I was maybe five or six years old I distinctly remember riding in the car with my mother when we came upon an accident on Broad Street in Rome. A young lady had fallen from an automobile when the car door had flown open mid-turn. She was thrown from the car to the asphalt. This was before the requirement of seat belts. My mother reacted so quickly. She pulled our car over to the side and, still in her nurse's uniform, raced over to provide assistance. It was like watching a superhero as I peered over the large dashboard. Even to this day I believe that nurses are superheroes.

I realize now that my parents were feminist in a profound, and previously undefined, way. I don't remember any time that I didn't inherently think of both my mother and my father as equals. Regardless of society, religion, or any other dogma, it was a value in the truest sense of the word and it wasn't until I was older that I could actually appreciate both my parents' ability to define the ideal through the way they lived their lives.

My father was an insurance salesman with brief sojourns in car sales and retail. He was a World War II veteran having served with the corps of engineers. He was authoritative, loved to sing, worked hard, and had a quick wit. It's my father's pedigree that connects us to John Chandler, the first Chandler to come to America in 1610 on a ship named the *Hercules*. It was a little known fact that I discovered much later with the help of DNA testing and The Chandler Family Association. My father said a good prayer and he could tell a good joke. He remembered everyone he came into contact with and was generous to a fault.

Our family went through phases of bible study, sometimes frequently and other times more sporadically. We spent a lot of time at church and we shared dinner every night at home together. In our home we didn't use the language of racial bigotry, we didn't play it loose with the Lord's name, and swearing was an occasional "damn" when my father had reached his limit with something, probably me. My favorite antic, when I figured it out, was to proclaim from another room the words "GOT DOWN" (say it out loud and you'll know what it sounds like) followed by "AND I COULDN'T GET UP!" My parents certainly reprimanded me, but I think they laughed on the inside at my pushing of the envelope.

I was a hyperactive child. And this was before Ritalin or the practice of child therapy. I had an unfiltered comical streak full of impressions, jokes, pranks, and often-obnoxious rambling. I craved attention. I was imaginative and irreverent. My hyperactivity, my love for the completely absurd, and my inclination for "shock value" in humor were tolerated until I was old enough for it to become an embarrassment to those close to me. That turn of events changed a lot of things and probably contributed to my ongoing confusion as to what is acceptable and what is not. For a long time the line to cross kept moving beneath me and I was constantly looking down…and back.

I don't think my parents really knew what to do with me. I was creative and sensitive, yet determined and strong willed. I was the youngest of three children and craved the spotlight. Now, being the "baby" of three children could be the best seat in the house. I got attention without a lot of the restrictions. And when things weren't going my way—operating full throttle and energetically—I questioned every rule, reprimand, or direction. My imagination dictated my actions often and I had an underdeveloped ability to think ahead. And I got punished…a lot. Now I don't mean spanked, I mean full on leather-belt-to-the-bare-bottom whipped. I was born in 1959 and in our world of farm-descendent discipline, religious devotion, and assumed etiquette, my attempts at pushing boundaries and inquisitive folly did not always bode well. My father was the disciplinarian and if I said the wrong thing or misbehaved I could be instructed to retrieve the leather belt and go to the bathroom. I would wait in silence. Sometimes I would be bold enough to run from him and other times I could conjure devices to help me through the punishment. I would check my bare behind in the mirror after my father left to look at the immediately sore red-purple bruises. Sometimes sitting in my desk the next day at school was painful and the thought never occurred to me to tell anyone. It just wasn't something one did at that time. And I knew that I had misbehaved, but didn't understand how to control my actions or my sarcasm. And more than the pain or bruising, I think I was most impacted by the rage that it takes for someone to hit another person. I was much too aware of my father's fury and it made me harbor my own anger and resentment. I often heard the adage, "This hurts me much more than it hurts you," which, at the time, made absolutely no sense. Knowing my parents as an adult I could begin to understand that they might have genuinely meant it. Later it would become clear to me that they were caught in the struggle to change an age-old pattern of punishment handed down through generations of a particular way of thinking. I was new territory. And, like any child, the thought of my parent's disappointment was more disheartening than any punishment.

Years later, in one of our many late night conversations, I would discuss these incidents with my father. Now I was older and had a stronger grasp of the subject. My father was genuinely remorseful and was extremely honest with me. It was a different time. Parents and elders spanked children, sometimes with a hand, a switch, or sometimes a belt. A pop across the face wasn't unusual in response to a smart-aleck remark. And I never knew how my parents could elastically extend their arms across the dinner table or from the front seat of the car. I don't condone it, but that's what it was. This kind of punishment had existed for years. But now, I wanted my dad to know that I understood why it existed and that I was acutely aware of the moment he changed his opinion and altered his own behavior. He did the best he could and when he knew better, he did better. Now, if only society could do the same.

In many ways I knew my father as two different people. And the father I came to know as I grew older would become my hero and my biggest supporter. His ability to change his opinion on a variety of subjects and accept me for who I was served as a comfort and a lesson to me. For my father, I was an entirely new concept of a male child complete with artistic sensibility and outrageousness. As I grew older and was able to focus (at least a bit), he would come to see that it was possible for me to harness my own personality.

I think my father also recognized his own conflicted sides. He was an army veteran. He had a strong work ethic. He was a deacon at the church, well known throughout the community, and had a fun loving sense of humor. My dad reminded me of Dick Van Dyke and his humor struck the familiar chords of the comedians of the day including Don Rickles and Carl Reiner. I was a typical kid who would commence the eye rolls when he took the spotlight, but at the same time laugh on the inside while I observed his ability to hold the attention of the people around him.

I also watched as my father cared for my mother for sixteen years as she battled the slow and painful affects of Alzheimer's. My father honored his marital vows with his definition of what being a husband and partner would mean, and a deep dedication to his spiritual beliefs. I had seen my mother care for people through the nursing profession and now the roles were being reversed as she slipped into the veil of unknowingness. My father was resolute in his intention to care for my mother. It would break my heart to see him take a brief moment to walk out into the backyard to break down in tears. He would steady himself and take a breath. I watched his steps, one foot in front of the other, making his way back into the house. I had never witnessed that kind of strength, care, and yes, love. That's how my father would become my hero.

And now, a story about socks…

In an effort to curb what I now know was an awareness of my feminine side; my father decided I should spend time at the local Boys Club of America. It was a safe place for me and I alternated between watching television with nerdy types and learning to play sports with athletic types. The advantage of being a small, skinny, "Sears-Roebuck slim section" kind of kid is that I could be fast. I was agile, flexible, and I had speed. So I began to play basketball. It was also another way that I could emulate my brother's athleticism and hopefully impress. As fate would have it, I was placed on one of the third-grade teams during basketball season. I enjoyed it and resided without consequence until one particular game. I wanted desperately to look like one of the older kids with their basketball uniforms and their striped athletic socks. I enthusiastically dressed for the Saturday game and searched my brother's drawers for some uniform socks with stripes. My mother dropped me off at the Club only aware of my top layer of clothing that was sweat pants and a jacket. My father and my brother arrived for our game to watch me play and I was sure this would be a moment where they could see me behaving "appropriately" and acting in a manner that they had stressed, over and over, was exactly how a boy should behave. There were no official uniforms just gym clothes. But even then I was conscious of my makeshift basketball uniform.

I had carefully dressed myself in a pair of gym shorts that were much too large, probably worn too high on my waist and unable to fit my teeny bird-like legs. I wore a white T-shirt that a friend of my cousin's had embodied with a cartoon. It was a picture of a Tasmanian devil. The artwork clearly drawn with the words "Little Monster" carefully crafted into the design. *Yes, Lady Gaga, I was wearing a "Little Monster" T-shirt in the sixties!* I had found the perfect pair of green socks with white stripes at the top and laced up my converse sneakers and took to the court. Imagine a pint-sized "Barney Fife." The game flew by and I even recall a couple of good plays on my part.

The game ended and we loaded the car for the drive home. Silence. *Why weren't they congratulating me? Why no reaction from the very two people I was seeking approval from?* Finally my brother couldn't hold it in any longer and he turned from the front seat to confront me.

"What are you wearing?"

"What?" I questioned. I was perplexed.

He continued with the sharp line of interrogation. "Where did you get those socks?"

"In your sock drawer. What's wrong?" I replied still confused by the hostility.

Now prepare yourself for the kicker…

My brother informed me "Scott, those are baseball socks!"

What the hell? I had no clue. I knew they were a little big for me and I knew they were riding high above my knees but I thought this was perfectly acceptable. I had no idea those nifty athletic socks I saw the older kids wearing didn't have stirrups. Hell, I didn't even know what a stirrup was. Here I was in baggy gym shorts, a "Little Monster" T-shirt and… THIGH HIGHS!

The embarrassment from the front seat of the car began to fill up the back seat like rising water in the bowels of a sinking ship. Needless to say that was my last basketball game or at least the last basketball game I remember playing. I don't even know if I returned to the Boys Club. If I did it was probably all television and Krystal burgers from there on out.

OK, I think this story is hilarious now, but at the time it was pretty devastating. Throughout the years I've told the story many times and the art of self-deprecation has made me stronger. The art of owning one's missteps is a valuable and revealing tool. Even when it includes thigh highs.

The confusion and the contradictions would continue. My mother always said I was twirling the cardboard part of a clothes hanger at a very early age. I would mimic the majorettes from the high school band. *Imagine if I had a male baton twirling role model? What if I could have seen those dynamo drum majors from Ohio State University?* It was fine to twirl a cheap baton for the amusement of the majorettes, the high school band kids, or a local talent show until I reached the age when my peers, and particularly boys, took notice. Baton was a "girl" thing right? The trouble started. It didn't take long before my brother, six years older, would break the batons in half and the name-calling started. It was cute for a flexible little kid to dance around copying the dancers on television shows until the teacher had to call my parents to inform them that I had been dancing my way to the pencil sharpener. My teacher was not amused. I was distracting…and confused. I performed imitations and little monologues. I could sing an accent-infused Tammy Wynette "D-I-V-O-R-C-E" to everyone's delight, but I had trouble understanding the time and place. I certainly didn't understand how it could entertain some people and others would disapprove. My report cards were riddled with unsatisfactory marks in discipline, self-control, and behavior. The disapproval carried over to my male classmates and thus began the daily humiliation that would last until I was old enough to engage survival tactics.

I experienced a constant barrage of names like "sissy, homo, queer bait, faggot." The words, like daggers, were a daily reminder that I was somehow different. I developed a nervous stomach and would sit through classes, clenched fist digging into my leg, struggling to fight the pain. This kind of daily humiliation continued for years, even through high school.

And when I say daily, I really do mean it was every single day. Imagine hearing the verbal venom and not knowing exactly what it actually meant. You learn where and when to move from class to class. You learn who to avoid and how not to make eye contact. You learn when to arrive and when to depart. You learn how to feign illness in order to leave school early to avoid the after school threat. Learning to navigate the labyrinth of my instincts and my humiliation was a trial every day. It's not easy and it's not comfortable. I experienced more confusion every day.

At the same time I had a few friends who provided a safe place to be myself. I had no idea what any of it all meant and certainly wasn't old enough to know what it meant sexually. But amid the snubbing, taunting, shoving, and threats, I was on constant alert. I was nervous and oblivious. It could make me physically sick to my stomach. I was ashamed, but hiding behind humor when I thought I was safe. And here's the thing about being a bullied kid—you can't always go home and talk to your parents or tell a teacher because you're not sure whether they feel exactly the same as your oppressors. You are afraid. Your biggest fear is thinking that the very people you want to help you might actually condemn you.

I was a sensitive kid and it wasn't difficult to detect the disdainful conflict my parents or my brother were feeling. There was no place to express the anguish. So I was an endless series of attempts to bring back whatever it was that had garnered approval in the past—all without knowing that, as I got older none of the past would suffice anyway. I really would not have survived if I had not enjoyed the company of a few really good friends throughout the years that, although we never spoke of it, clearly understood and allowed me my personality. Our particular church was a safe place because of the reverence and disciplined services, and perhaps because of some progressively minded adults. I knew better than to exercise any kind of disobedience at church. It wasn't until my teenage years that religion would force a startling new set of questions.

And then there was my sister Susan. Thirteen years my senior, Susan had been like a mother to me when both our parents were working. She never judged my personality, my behavior, or my talent and she witnessed first hand the plight of my grammar school existence. One summer break, we went swimming at a local pool and would have been the only ones there that morning had it not been for one of my classmates and his older brother. They began by making circles around us. In the pool and out of the pool, taunting us, shouting the names I heard on a daily basis. They were splashing, throwing things, and continuing the humiliating hunt until we were reduced to a huddle holding onto the side of the pool. I was devastated. My sister shielded me as best she could, asking me, "Are you OK?" They finally tired of their game and my sister never spoke of it again. What may seem so silly as an adult can be traumatic for a child. But Susan understood and the bond we shared remained another anchor that I could often hold fast to when times were tough. When I did, years later, open up to my sister in a "coming out" letter, she fought off the tears as she told me how much she hated the pain that I had experienced. Her acknowledgement of my experience was an important moment for me.

I started piano lessons in the first grade and continued for four years. It was another much-needed escape. A kid taking piano lessons was something that my parents understood and supported even though they were not musicians themselves. But once again, being diligent at studies would prove difficult. It was difficult to sit still and concentrate, and the urge to exercise my own creativity could be a problem. I could easily play by ear. My piano teacher began to recognize it after my first year. I could follow her demonstrations easily and play them back to her. Her attempts to alter this unique ability were unsuccessful and her frustration at my lack of technical diligence was apparent. She was a kind lady, but yes: She used a ruler for keeping time and sometimes a tap on the knuckles. Before long my hyperactivity won out over my ability to become a serious, focused student. It makes sense to me now that what I truly needed was the opportunity to make music <u>and</u> motion at the same time. I needed marching music.

The seesaw of emotional highs and lows continued throughout grammar school. In the middle of troublesome behavior issues, there would be interesting enlightenment from a couple of progressive teachers. Mrs.

Moore was my fourth-grade teacher and her husband was a challenging, controversial teacher at the high school that my brother attended. He had encouraged his students to read the New York Times bestseller, *The Greening of America*. A sociological examination of sixtie's counterculture, the book was a strong contrast to the conservative nature of our southern town. I may have the facts wrong on the story, but I was aware of the controversy whether Mr. Moore had assigned the book or not. I knew my brother read it and it was discussed openly in our home (and obviously among conservative school board members). I don't know the end result of the controversy or whatever happened to Mr. Moore, but it gives you an idea of what free thinkers this husband and wife were. The openness trickled down to our tiny fourth-grade class through Mrs. Moore's encouragement that all of us have an opinion. It's the first time I ever remember being allowed or encouraged to have an opinion on any subject that wasn't a bicycle color or pet parakeet names. She would offer a variety of subjects from books we might be reading to current events. We were free and completely able to say what we were thinking. I will never forget that and, most of all, how she treated us with respect even though she knew how limited we might be. Mrs. Moore also asked me to bring a baton to school. She put on music and I performed for the class. She did the same with several students and their various talents. What I don't think she comprehended was the reaction of some of the boys, and sometimes girls, in the class. There was encouragement on the one hand, and disapproval on the other. More contradiction. More confusion.

Mrs. Chappell, my fifth-grade teacher, really "got" me and remains my favorite memory of elementary school. She was a creative, bohemian type who would cover the chalkboard in multi-colored chalk drawings of psychedelic flowers and curvilinear designs. We were encouraged to do the same in whatever way invigorated our fancy. My imagination was flourishing and she took a special interest in my artistic expression and even gave me special assignments that would illustrate different projects that she was pursuing. She brought her son, a toddler at the time, into the classroom and we were allowed to play and watch his reactions. We were allowed to be kids and she still had a unique ability to keep the class in complete control.

Now if I were a choreographer of some monumental stature, what I'm about to tell you would be a great story. But however my tiny piece of the world may be, this was an important moment for me. For a class project that I can't even recall, Mrs. Chappell charged me with a small group of students, complete with raincoats and umbrellas, to create my very first act of choreography with the song "Raindrops Keep Falling on My Head." *Ah yes, Burt Bacharach.* Now I have no idea how I concocted a count structure or changing forms, or better yet, taught my classmates to manipulate the umbrellas to open and close in time to the music. I didn't know how to create a sense of pacing and musicality, but in my primitive, innocent way, I made it happen. I simply remember that it occurred and I remember that it worked. I have no idea whether it was good or showcased any quality, but I remember it as an "event" and I remember that feeling of accomplishment and Mrs. Chappell's approval. I'm sure I had watched enough television with The June Taylor Dancers, the musical numbers on *The Carol Burnett Show*, or award show production numbers to fake it in my undeveloped process. I innately knew how to let the fantasy take over and "pretend" my way through. Somehow it was natural for me and somehow Mrs. Chappell recognized my aptitude and, better yet, my interest.

Among my stories of superb teachers is an incident from sixth grade. Mrs. Payne, Mrs. Chappell, Mrs. O'Brien, and Mrs. Beasley were four teachers who shared the quadrant of classrooms that made up our fifth and sixth grades. They were a diverse group of women who cared deeply for all the students and worked together to offer us the very best education. We rotated from classroom to classroom for different subjects throughout the day: Mrs. Beasley, quiet, gentle, and unassuming; Mrs. O'Brien with her intelligent manner and her cardigan draped collegiately over her shoulders; Mrs. Chappell, the free-spirited bohemian and my idol; Mrs. Payne with a celebrity-like personality that entertained and educated at the same time. One time Mrs. Payne even promised that if everyone in the class achieved a certain score on a spelling test that she would stand on her head and whistle "Dixie." Guess what? We did! And she fulfilled her promise to the absolute delight of everyone. She actually wore pants to school that day and kept her promise.

On one typical morning just like any other day, Mrs. Beasley was away from our homeroom during the morning routine of The National Anthem and the recitation of The Pledge of Allegiance. Being left to our own devices in our separate room was license to "thrill" for an amusing collection of sixth graders. We began to recite the pledge in animated voices with varying degrees of volume. The longer we continued the more exaggerated we became. We moved and sang to the anthem and before long the other teachers could hear the noise erupting from our boisterous room. They descended on our classroom like a SWAT team. We were in trouble—BIG trouble. But here's the kicker: the punishment we expected came in a uniquely challenging form that took us by complete surprise. These four intelligent, inventive women charged us with creating a short play that would explain the story of The Pledge of Allegiance and the Star Spangled Banner. So this mixture of adolescent buffoonery had to create something as a team even through the groans and discontent of several students. But we did it, with their guidance of course, and presented our little slice of theatre to the other homerooms. I played Francis Scott Key because of our shared name (of course) and we were costumed, rehearsed, and actually learned something from the experience. At least I did. What could have resulted in a cold, menacing code of punishment that would go unnoticed, and soon be forgotten, was reinvented to make us think. And it was another example of underpaid teachers, caring and intelligent, using each and every opportunity to do the most important thing they could ever do…educate.

In the sixth grade students began to learn music on song flutes. I instantly related to the process and was drawn to the notion of taking up an instrument. I was already obsessed with the older kids in the high school marching band so I knew that I would soon have my own chance. Looking back, I can say it's something like the sorting hat scene in a Harry Potter film. For me, a small, energetic, wide-eyed devotee, the day could not come fast enough. Again my parents, even without any prior experience of their own, would support my enthusiasm. Merchants from a local music store brought a variety of instruments into a small room at the elementary school. I felt as if I were walking into a museum. I was allowed to test out each instrument while the adult supervisors would operate the instrument to produce what I thought were the most magical of sounds. Upon completion I was told what instruments I might be proficient at and the appropriate note was sent home to my parents. We would have to make a choice for this first step. I had options from the big bore mouthpieces of the trombone or baritone to the smaller brass instruments of trumpet or French horn. The saxophone was on the list and I even recall the oboe on the list and was amazed at its snake charmer sound.

I wanted to play the French horn but had to choose trombone. My father informed me, after what was probably a little research on his part, that we could not afford a French horn. I think he had, with his connections throughout the community, stumbled upon on a used trombone that he could actually pay for. I didn't mind it at all. I loved the sound and the tricks the trombone slide could produce.

What I did not think about was the fact that, as a student that walked to school every day, the trombone and it's larger case was pretty much the same size as my meager frame. It was not the best idea for a kid who could find himself running home to escape the non-musically inclined. Nevertheless, I thrived and persevered.

Seventh grade and a move across the street to junior high would bring a new experience, and a new mixture of students from the local area. I was thrilled for a chance to start over and meet other students from a variety of backgrounds. The stories of a changing racial climate and the challenges of women and minorities were no longer just topics on the news or discussions between my parents at the dinner table. It was real and happening before our eyes and the plights of all kinds of people became a reality and a history that I would want to understand in a personal way.

The same people I had suffered through my previous school with were present, but at least the world was getting a little bigger. And I would have to learn quickly to control my anger and resentment even though I was totally unaware of why it could appear at any given moment. I began to "talk back" as the adults would say. I challenged authority and I harbored a rebellious nature not only for myself, but also for the air of social injustice that was ever present. I wanted new friends and I craved acceptance and that could lead to harsh punishment from teachers also.

Mrs. Askew, one of my teachers, had no tolerance for my bad timing or my gregarious personality. She chose one particular morning to unleash her anger when I was having a laugh with a new friend during class. I received her full wrath and she publicly declared me a "sissy" and to stop "acting like a girl." On another similar occasion, she brought me to the front of the class and brought out the wooden board to paddle my backside. It was a public punishment. It was fuel for the fire to the bullies in the room. My friend surprisingly wasn't reprimanded and I hope this kind of retribution doesn't occur now. Sadder still was the fact that I really admired Mrs. Askew. She had a large personality and an air of confidence that I worshipped. That is, until she showed this different side of herself. I'm afraid for any young person, lost inside his or her own self-discovery, to be the victim of an adult who does not take the time to consider the story behind the student. Every student has a story.

Smaller than most of my peers, I was an easy target. Somehow I kept testing the boundaries and would think that I could find some sort of acceptance from the bully types. And on one occasion I found myself in the middle of a game of toss. The problem was that I was the one being tossed. Airborne until I would hit the ground only to be rustled back up again, all amid the barrage of name-calling and laughter. It was dog piling and kicking and humiliation. And just like punishment from parents, the worst part is the anger behind the actions. The tone of the hatred and sheer disgust is incomprehensible. Luckily I wasn't seriously hurt before the principal arrived at the wooded area in front of the school where the event occurred. The boys were immediately directed to his office and I slowly walked back into the school trying to recover some kind of dignity. And here's where my tenacity melted into my ignorance. I really thought that if I said it was "no big deal," they would suddenly treat me differently. I made my way to the office and offered an explanation to the principal that it was all in "good fun." Even though I knew that underneath it all was an unkind, power play at my expense. I never knew what happened to those boys. Perhaps nothing. And it didn't help my cause. The relationships didn't change. It would only serve as another instance of picking myself up and moving forward.

Here's a quick aside to illustrate how confusing a time this would be. Physical Education was a required class. Depending on the season of the year, our gender-separated classes were required to "dress out" in gym clothes and participate in a given sport. Spring would be softball. Imagine my fear. Sports were my brother's thing and, per the infamous basketball story, we know I might not be intrinsically aware of how this would work. Coach Tarpley was in charge of the class. Maybe it was a cruel joke or he had actually seen some potential in me, but I was delegated to the position of pitcher. I had no idea how to pitch beyond whatever Coach Tarpley had previously explained. This was going to go one of two ways. I was either going to survive it or be the poster child for Irritable Bowel Syndrome. It's seventh grade, I'm basically a runt, a lot of these other boys spend way too much of their time getting attention at my expense, and I reeked of fear. I was an easy target. It's all fodder for disaster.

Surprisingly, I excelled. I was striking batters out left and right. I faced a fear and it probably threw every one off their game. Coach Tarpley would put my name on a poster mounted in the classroom as the "Star Player" for the week on more than one occasion. I know the coach had to be aware of my social predicament. And I think about this all these years later with a deep admiration for that coach and my own perseverance. Find the tiniest of moments and use them as fuel.

My refuge was always the music department. The junior high school band director was a wise gentlemanly figure named Herman Scott. He was respectful, taught us well, and genuinely cared for all his students. He would clarify his proclamation that we were acting like fools in our moments of noisy rambunctiousness. He would, in his dignity, let us know that he meant fools with a "ph," not fools with an "f." He was not going to let any moment lower his standards of respect for any human being, no matter the age, and somehow this ever-so-slight change of lettering altered the implication.

The music program would keep me in school throughout my education and I would bet there are a multitude of students all around the world who could say the same. Band, and particularly marching band for me, provided a place to reside as part of a team. I could express my talents, my enjoyment—and the discipline of this particular focus worked well for me. Even with the conflicts, music would keep me showing up for school each and every day. The safety of the music programs I experienced also allowed me to explore the art and theatre departments. It broadened my horizons, gave me dreams and began to offer me a method by which to learn how to control myself. It guided me to new parts of the library and as a result, the world outside my hometown. I could dream of other places. I could dream of theatre, or dance, or painting. It became my realization that no matter how some people were attacking me throughout my daily existence that there was a forward motion taking me somewhere beyond.

I proceeded one foot in front of the other.

My freshmen and sophomore years of high school were revolving more and more around church and religion. I was becoming more aware of myself and even though I didn't fully understand what being gay meant I was certainly aware of my feelings. So I retreated into church and its many activities. For some reason I never suffered at our own church, even though I'm sure the judgment existed. In addition to uncles that were pastors, I would witness some church members that I still consider truly spiritual, caring, genuine examples of what our religion professed.

I prayed nightly, as so many people have, to be delivered from my so-called "affliction." I knew that if I was diligent and disciplined that all these thoughts and feelings would disappear. Until, that is, several of us decided to attend a weeklong revival/workshop for teenagers at one of the larger local churches.

The Life Action Singers came to town and after a fee, provided us with a workbook and a series of lessons each day—and we were allowed to miss school for the week. One particular day we entered the church sanctuary to the music of Elton John. I was immediately thrilled. *Were they actually going to approve of this secular music that I obviously enjoyed? Were they going to embrace some kind of youthful exuberance from the outside world? Was this*

OK that we listened to this? Of course we all did anyway. Well, nothing could be further from the truth. That day's emphasis became a bully pulpit that would proclaim our wrongful ways and the perils of popular music. And it did not stop there. At one point the evangelical speaker, full of stereotypical fire and brimstone, made an unforgettable statement.

"... I know some of you are homosexuals. I can see it on your faces. Your faces are red right now because you know I'm talking about you!"

I was mortified. I was totally horrified, ashamed, and degraded. Here I was, amid my unspoken struggle, sitting among some of the very same people who had made my life a living hell, listening to an authority figure supposedly speaking the word of God and throwing the biggest stone at me. *Could this be right? Is this kind of public humiliation really what being a Christian is about?* I couldn't move. My stomach pain returned. And I was flooded with the very guilt that this inane egomaniacal bigot had desired. *My face is so red right now.* I was crushed and it was building up inside of me. At the end of the sermon the offer was made, as is common, for members of the congregation to come forward and get guidance and counseling in the choir room behind the baptismal pool. Different teens, for a multitude of reasons I'm sure, made their way down the aisle to the back where the counselors waited. I finally gave in. I made my way to the strains of the music specifically designed to provoke this kind of response. *Theatre anyone?* I made my way to the choir room and collapsed into a chair and began to cry. Everything from the past and the present was manifesting in my anguish. I was a ball of confusion. I looked at the counselors, some consoling other teenagers, some waiting with Bibles in hand, and I glanced at a clock on the wall through my hands as I sat alone and cried. I sobbed and knew that one way or another this was going to be a release.

No one ever came over.

I waited.

It was half an hour to forty-five minutes, but it felt much longer when I finally looked around the room to discover that there were still some of these so-called disciples talking among themselves.

Not one of them ever came over.

Let the swearing begin. *Don't repeat what you were really thinking.*

I was angry.

My life changed that day. My thoughts about God, or a higher power, or the universe, or whatever this thing is that is bigger than all of us, did NOT change one bit. But that very moment would begin my journey, as difficult as it can be, to aspire to just be a better version of myself. I may not have known what I was feeling, but I knew that I was worth more than this kind of treatment. And I knew that whatever God is, God made me just as I am.

And I am not alone.

Unfortunately for me, I was living in a cultural climate that supported the actions of those who took it upon themselves to declare me "something" that I didn't really understand. Other people were defining me. I was a young person in the process of discovery. I didn't know who to talk to or even what to say if I did. I found refuge where I could. I gravitated to a few friends who did not carry judgmental, prejudice, or ignorant belief.

If you are being mistreated or bullied...

Fortunately now, there are many more understanding adults, peers, and resources for information on what you are feeling and how to navigate the emotional terrain. Now a person can go online and research or find phone numbers to call and speak with someone. There is help and there is hope. Young people need to know that. No matter the degree to which you may feel unfairly judged or treated, you can talk about it and get help. Don't ever think you're being silly. Know that any feeling you have is real. If you are making mistakes, you will learn and correct them. If you have questions, there are answers out there. And if something you read or someone you talk to makes you feel in the slightest bit unworthy, then begin your search again. You are worth it.

CHAPTER 2

You Dream (a Lot)

I spent four years with a high school band director who was a master of the negative comment with a constant power play to exert control over me. Granted, I was not the easiest student. Eager, enthusiastic, constantly questioning, and continually craving attention, I was needy. I had grown up on the defensive for a number of obvious reasons, not the least of which was being gay, and nothing could stop my genuine test of the limits and the desire to figure out what I was feeling. For the first two years I was quiet, diligent, and anxious to learn everything possible. Then I slowly became a bit more confident. My mind raced with ideas much faster than I could understand or filter. I grew up in a time and a place where, for whatever reason, there was no definition of who I was or what I was experiencing. No role models. No exposure to what was really happening with the brave pioneers charting new territory with honesty, defiance, and strength for who and what they really were as human beings. I was a kid who could be perfect one second and disobedient the next. My manners could be exemplary and shift to the rebellious in a flash. I was a teenager. And I forever wanted to move forward—to find something new.

I did learn a lot from this talented man, especially when it came to jazz and improvisation, but I could never find that security that comes with a true mentor. You know the teacher that can give you the negative or the positive and you feel like he or she is unconditionally on your side? Not this man, and not with me. Perhaps he was a different teacher with other students and now that I'm older I understand if he couldn't figure out the puzzle that was my personality.

Regardless, I still spent the majority of my time in the band room—the music department. It essentially was my life throughout high school. I learned a lot, but that department also benefited from my creativity and my imagination. I wrote flag routines. I wrote drill formations. I was drum major for two years and learned a great deal from summer drum major camps, incidentally at Jacksonville State University in nearby Jacksonville, Alabama. Jacksonville State University would prove to be a pivotal experience for me in the not too distant future.

One year at our own summer band camp I completely changed the marching style when the band director was away for a family crisis. I taught a drum corps style marching technique that I had learned at drum major camp as opposed to the more traditional high leg lift we historically performed. The change made sense to me and I had previously requested that we adapt the new style to no avail. Back then there was no marching band staff and we weren't a large school. When he returned, the director relented even though his resentment was more than obvious. I was scolded and lectured but there was no time to turn back with the first performance quickly approaching. We would unveil our updated style at the first football game. Fortunately, there was nothing but support for our new technique. And incidentally, they still use the updated style to this day. I had a strong conviction and I knew I had the support of fellow members and I also knew that this strong-willed man wasn't foreign to progressive thinking. He was a brilliant jazz player and my time alternating from trombone to piano to vocals in our jazz ensemble was a significant learning experience that I truly cherish. But the personal relationship was an entirely different story and even my parents, after chaperoning a couple of band trips, acknowledged my angst over the relationship that added to an already turbulent period. Observing him on a daily basis was enough to convince me that I could never be a band director. And I certainly was given the idea that it would not be the best route for me.

Years later I would encounter this same high school director while I was working with the Spirit of Atlanta Drum and Bugle Corps. I think he was genuinely impressed and seemed like a much more relaxed person. I like to think he had changed and wouldn't be the same teacher I had endured. *Where were you all those years ago?* I also like to think I had gained a thicker skin and could actually listen more. We all evolve.

Things would begin to shift during my junior year of high school and I began to gain a better sense of timing. Among peers, I was becoming aware of how to speak and when to remain silent; what to wear and how to avoid the danger zones; when to push the boundaries and when to blend into the crowd. I learned about survival and even though I was still making mistakes and bad decisions (note the pants tucked inside a pair of boots), I was becoming more and more aware of how to maneuver the landscape of adolescence. I studied magazines and *Soul Train*. I could listen to Roberta Flack or Led Zeppelin. I was holding fast to the friends I had and even gained support from upper classmen. When I had no friends I lived in my imagination. I was occasionally dating girls and not completely convinced that what I felt on the inside wasn't just a passing phase.

Times are so different now for young people discovering their sexuality and I am thankful for those that have boldly made that possible. Unfortunately, that kind of awareness didn't exist for us in the seventies in our "in-between" town. And my exploration wasn't leading me to the truth about great artists, musicians, writers, or the many men and women who braved the Stonewall riots. This was teenage purgatory. My fantasy world revolved around books of plays in the library or articles in *The New Yorker*. I read a copy of *The Boys in the Band* in a compilation of the year's plays that somehow slipped into our highly guarded library collection. It scared me. And it still wasn't a reflection of the life I was living. Thus furthering my obliviousness that one label did not fit every person or life.

When rumors would surface about another student I understood them exercising their own individuality but couldn't always relate to the end product. I wasn't a boy who wore make-up. I didn't dress in women's clothes. I didn't want to be a girl. I didn't pass any judgment on those unique people either. I thought they were simply expressing themselves, yet I immediately related to their persecution. I admired their individualism, but it wasn't necessarily what I was feeling. I couldn't see my own effeminate qualities or hear the inflections that others could point out, but I was also learning how to manipulate the door of my own "closet." Learning to live a duality, I could alter the tone of my voice or walk with a different weight to my step, suffering the limitations, yet appreciating a sense of inclusion.

My moments of loneliness became an opportunity to daydream and create. I could enter a fantasy world and pass the hours playing music, sketching, or writing. And I loved watching television. Field trips to museums or theatres in Atlanta would keep reminding me that something was buzzing beyond the Floyd County line. I saw Calder mobiles and Shakespeare. I saw tall buildings and the bustling interstate. I watched the Falcons and the Braves. My parents even took me to the Ryman Auditorium in Nashville, Tennessee. The Grand Ole Opry in all its glory with the live music, and the sea of beehive hairdos in the audience, and the hilarity of Minnie Pearl. Tiny moments were giving me huge ideas. I knew there was more.

One night in 1976 my father called me from the family room of our small three-bedroom home to let me know there were marching bands on the television. I rushed from my room to the den. There on PBS, was the Drum Corps International Championships. My father, mother, and I watched the entire broadcast amazed and spellbound by the excitement, precision, and skills being performed. For me, impressionable and confined, if something was on television it obviously was important. Observing this kind of artistry and performance on a television broadcast legitimized my obsession. Here, with celebrity commentary, was the very thing I had spent so many years pursuing whether I was pretending to go to band camp in the backyard or marching in my high school band. I had never seen drum corps. No one else in my family was involved in marching band or color guard. This was an entirely new world and one that carried a level of professionalism that neither I, nor my parents, knew existed. Here it was, another life-changing experience, all because Drum Corp International had the wherewithal to jettison their art into the mainstream world. A significant moment materialized when the Madison Scouts of Madison, Wisconsin took to the field. Here was a group of performers—brass players, drummers, rifles, flags, and they were all male. The energy and the masculinity were beyond belief and the level of excellence was incredible. They weren't effeminate or "sissy" and they were in complete control. I think it changed my parent's thinking and it certainly altered my destiny. If that sounds dramatic so be it. It's the truth. I didn't know how or when, but I knew I had to be a part of it. When The Scouts finished their performance I told my parents that I would be a "Madison Scout" someday. My father stated through a chuckle, "You're not goin' off to Wisconsin." It's understandable that he would react that way because the whole idea was foreign. It didn't matter. I knew I would and I had no idea how or when it would happen.

My senior year went by without too many troublesome incidents. I was gaining better self-control and even though it was an existence of hiding parts of myself, I was able to understand more clearly that I may not have all the answers yet. It wasn't always fair and I knew that it wasn't right, but there was a distinct sense of hope that somewhere in the world there would be a place I could exist. As I learned more about history I was realizing how much denial, persecution, and outright injustice had occurred time and time again. I contemplated example after example of the ignorance and lack of empathy on the part of one group turning righteous indignation towards another group of human beings. *Is it human nature? Does it ever change? Will it always exist? How did the survivors of those horrific episodes make it through to another existence? Does right always win out in the end?* This was a long list of deep and intense questions for a teenager, but I had a sense that I couldn't be alone in this. There were people out there who were just like me and it was only a matter of time before I could find them.

I continued in the music department, acted in theatre productions, and relished my time with my art teacher. I was selective about the people I spent time with and I cherished their friendships. I traded my desire to emulate Rod Stewart for the conservative Levi's and topsiders. I repressed my inner David Bowie knowing full well the Thin Duke persona would probably play more like some *Hee-Haw* wardrobe room disaster.

I don't remember exactly know how I met Jim Gladson. He was a music educator from across town, but had also instructed drum and bugle corps with big names like The Troopers and The Oakland Crusaders. He had a rich history in the marching arts. If I've learned anything about drum corps and color guard people, it's that we don't mind spending endless hours talking about this unique activity. When we stumble upon someone who actually knows and understands it, we don't mind discussing and extolling the attributes of all it encompasses. We are a worldwide community of people who often enjoy and need the company of like minds.

I was able to visit with Jim at his school where he would show me movies and videos of various drum and bugle corps and indoor competitive color guards pre-music soundtrack. He saw my potential and even gave me some basic lessons in spinning (or twirling as some might say) a rifle. I began to master double-time spins, which are exactly like it sounds. The rifle spinning to quarter-note time could suddenly, through manipulation and technique, double the time. It was a miracle to behold for me and was amazing to watch and, more importantly, to master. Then he began to instruct me on the art of aerials. Tossing the rifle into the air, releasing the equipment with just the right amount of finesse, to rotate any number of times. He taught me to perform my first "triple." That's three revolutions while the rifle is airborne. Another miracle. It sounds simple for people who have mastered the technique, but to kinetically dissect the process really is quite amazing. One hand guiding the upward motion while the other pushes downward to add the right amount of speed. In today's contemporary color guards, rifles are tossed to dizzying heights and astounding rotations that can exceed upwards of seven or eight rotations or beyond. And now there is body involvement that creates an entirely new dimensionality. For me it all started with that "triple" and the kindness of Jim Gladson.

And now a story about my beautiful friend Tara…

I followed a group of my friends into a club called the Future Business Leaders of America. Now if you know me at all, business is not my forte. But the FBLA included commercial art and that was an area in which I could relate. Mrs. Boyles, the FBLA advisor and a wonderful teacher with an infectious laugh, suggested that another club member and I partner for a local competition in commercial art. Each team would be given a theme or slogan and would design a poster to advertise that marketing tool. Rest assured it always had something to do with "America." I could think quickly and my partner, Jennifer, had outstanding taste and could support the execution and clarity of the idea. We eventually won the competition through the state finals and would be making our way to the national convention to compete there. We would be traveling to Denver, Colorado for the National convention with several other students. The boys would share a room.

Tara was beautiful on the inside and out (and still is I'm sure). With her cheerleader enthusiasm and a lighthouse smile, she was friendly and caring to everyone she met. She embraced the comic side of herself and welcomed everyone into her circle. Tara was friendly with one of the boys attending the national convention and one could easily refer to him as "Mr. Everything". He was smart, intelligent, athletic, and handsome and definitely not my friend even though we had known each other since elementary school. Now this guy was not my idea of "Mr. Everything," and evidently didn't understand that I didn't admire him the way so many others did. *Whatever.* But somehow the story got back to me that he had declared his apprehension of rooming with me on the trip and definitely would not be sleeping in the same bed as me. He was sure I would make advances on him. Tara, with her crackpot sense of humor, had the best response.

She told him outright, "Don't flatter yourself!"

I thought it was the best response I had ever heard and I love Tara to this day for coming up with that one. We traveled to Denver and no, I did not sleep in the same bed with him and yes, we won the national competition. It was a win-win situation.

Let that be a lesson to "Mr. Everythings" everywhere. People, be they gay or women or whatever, do not always want to have sex with you. Don't assume the world is populated with people who aspire to be with you simply because you might be harboring a zeppelin-sized ego.

I can laugh about so many of those instances now. But I honestly think there were people and peers in my formative years that never knew my real name. I was addressed as "faggot" or "queer" and basically couldn't walk the hallways at school without hearing it at least once. Somehow, I white-knuckled the glimmer of a light at the end of the tunnel. I hung onto whatever would get me through the day. When I say it was a daily existence I am sincere about it. And that means either give into fear or somehow learn to choose my steps carefully. But learning to run that gauntlet was teaching me to compete.

The balance to my last high school years was a wonderful junior high music educator. Gene Inglis was intelligent, supportive, encouraging, and never let me feel that I was less than worthy. He was also an alumnus of JSU. He recognized my creativity and was the very definition of the word "teacher." I survived a lot because of Gene Inglis and my respect for him has grown over the years that I have spent around a multitude of music educators. I would recognize his generosity and professionalism when I joined the Jacksonville State University Marching Southerners and began to learn from an icon and a legend, Dr. David Walters.

CHAPTER 3

Momentum

I attended Jacksonville State University in Alabama on a theatre scholarship. It wasn't a full ride scholarship (or even close), but in 1977 theatre seemed like an ambitious, creative option for study when I became disillusioned with becoming a music educator or band director. Even though I was satiated with performing from an early age, I was drawn to music and marching in what I think was an extraordinary way. I was drawn to JSU not only for the theatre option, but also because of their renowned marching band, The Marching Southerners. I had seen them at High School marching band contests in exhibition and the level of excitement, entertainment, and excellence resonated with me in ways I could barely describe. So, of course I joined the Marching Southerners as well as pursuing a theatre major.

I thought I could do both, but evidently my college academic advisor didn't see it that way. He certainly didn't hide his disapproval of my involvement in areas beyond our theatre productions. A theatre professor himself, he may have had a valid point and had he not approached me from a "negative," I probably would have understood that I needed total focus and dedication to one area. Better yet, had he told me that I possessed the kind of potential that warranted that kind of dedication I might have paused to further examine my schedule. Here I was sitting within the concrete walls of his office and listening to his condescension and harboring the confusion of two opposing natural forces that couldn't seem to gel. He thought my participation in the marching band and the competitive indoor-color guard at JSU was well, "silly." I remember it clearly. I thought about that advisor years later as I walked around the Paramount lot for the first time contributing to *Glee*. Here I was, a part of bringing color guard to a musical television show about a group of kids who were alienated as outsiders in high school. I thought about his stern contempt again as I sat in a beautiful theatre in Nagoya, Japan preparing for the opening of the stage production of *Odyssey*.

Odyssey was commissioned and produced by the Min-On Organization in 2008. Similar to the Tony award–winning production *Blast!* but with an all-female cast and a poetic narrative full of experimental costuming, props, and lighting choices. It was an eye-opening experience, chaotic and beautiful at the same time. I wrote the book for the show, co-choreographed with the amazing Karl Lowe, designed the costumes, acted as director, and even contributed two original music compositions. Well received by audiences, it was a theatrical event that toured Japan and was a unique presentation of dance, marching music, and drama. Again theatre and musical pageantry would collide in a way that I would have never expected.

In many ways, life really began for me in the fall of 1977 at Jacksonville State University. For the very first time in my entire life, my day-to-day existence didn't revolve around avoiding certain people or disguising who I was in every single moment. I was free to express myself and feel, for the first time, acceptance in the real sense of the word. Being a part of The Marching Southerners was not only a dream experience, but also one that gave me a sense of pursuit that involved excellence, intensity, and enjoyment. I wasn't being trained with negative enforcement, but positive reinforcement. This made a huge difference for me. And the contrast to my high school experience couldn't have been more evident.

Dr. David Walters represented genius to me. He was the force behind this astonishing program at JSU and had also arranged music that was etched into the musical soundtrack that plays out in my head to this very day. Dr. Walters could also empower people to do their best work. Again, the contrast would serve as the lesson that we can always come out on the other side of any situation. The yin and the yang of it all has always let me know that no matter however bad the bad times can be, that's how good the good times can be. My experience with Dr. Walters and The Marching Southerners, well over three hundred members strong, was on the upside of all that is good. I belonged.

I started as a trombone player, but only performed a few games in that section of the band. Dr. Walters came to me and asked whether I would be interested in performing with the color guard. *Really? Are you kidding?* Boys were rare in most marching band color guards even though the very idea of color guard began with all males. There were four of us guys that Dr. Walters allowed to begin that new endeavor that has continued, and grown, to this day. I don't know the backstory to how this all came about. Drum and Bugle Corps were no strangers to all-male groups and that included male performers on rifle and flag-color guard. Perhaps the fact that The Southerners were full of "drums corps" performers versed in the most current trends and techniques would lead to this addition. Maybe it was the progressive nature of this inspired university program that would consider the timing right for this change. But for sure, it took a leap of faith from Dr. Walters to add boys to the color guard and I didn't hesitate to say yes. And once more, some strange twist of fate sent me on my way.

At the same time my classes and performances in the theatre department continued. Theatre history, acting, costume, lighting design, and dance fueled my resources and once again these two worlds would reside simultaneously. And no matter how many times I have come to the fork in the road that could have taken me in a new direction I have always returned to this place of pageantry that evidently is in my blood.

I caught a ride to JSU with a high school friend to attend band camp for the fall of 1977. Band camp is that time when marching band members begin learning the new season's show before classes start for the new semester. We arrived in Jacksonville and drove by the music building, Mason Hall. There, in a patch of green grass out front, were four guys with rifles performing choreography that I immediately recognized from The Madison Scouts Drum and Bugle Corps. It was the "Officer Krupke" routine from their previous competitive show and I stared through my passenger seat window as we passed slowly by their energetic re-creation of what I had only witnessed on television. It was like seeing movie stars. And one of those talented gentlemen would become my best friend, my collaborator and my brother…Tam Easterwood.

Deep breath.

I'm going to write the hardest part of this story first. And I'm going to cry. All these years later and I'm still crying. We lost Tam to a brain tumor in 1995. For all the people that Tam touched through his career as an educator, creator and friend, I could never do justice to his complete story. It's the same way I feel about my inept ability to truly convey the sixteen years that my mother battled Alzheimer's. People everywhere struggle with these issues and the agony of loss every single day and I am not the person to offer any kind of explanation. But the departure of these two people from my life has left me unbearably empty, and my pain remains something I am not totally ready to write about. Perhaps someday I will find a way. My comfort resides in the fact that I am better for having shared their lives. I learned from them and I learned from watching my father remain my mother's caregiver through those unbearably difficult years. My father's all-encompassing, total dedication to the care of my mother was heroic. He would never see it that way, but to me, it was epic and overwhelming.

I have always been a comical person, probably gaining that trait from my father's sociable antics. But I often think I lost my "funny" the day Tam died. The church in Holly Pond, Alabama where Tam grew up was completely over flowing with family, friends, students, and co-workers all in attendance to pay their respects. The night of the viewing I stood in the aisles of the church sanctuary just like everyone else and waited to take one last look at Tam. I honestly didn't know if this was something I could do. I made my way slowly following the traffic of mourners in the only manner I knew how…one foot in front of the other. I approached the casket and spoke with Tam's mother. I had a request; she approved and I placed a WGI Championship ring in the casket. It represented something that we both strived to achieve and it was a small way of giving something of myself to him with grateful adoration. He would have liked that gesture and I know it.

I literally ran from the church as quickly as I could and made my way to a private place outside in the darkness of the evening to break down. There I stood alone and looked up to see the bright stars in the night sky. Orion's Belt was clearly visible. To this day when I see that particular constellation I like to think he's looking out for me like the big brother/protector that he always was. And now I think Tam would tell me to get on with it.

FWD March

And now a story about a diaper…

The first musical I performed in at college was *Cabaret*. It was serendipitous. My favorite musical was, and still is, *Cabaret*. It's also my favorite movie and I wore the vinyl of the soundtrack within a millimeter of thread. I auditioned and was set to play the Emcee. Based on a book by Christopher Isherwood with music and lyrics by John Kander and Fred Ebb, there was a ghoulish, vaudeville-induced quality to the character of the emcee and I would have the opportunity to sing and dance. Pretty awesome for a freshmen theatre major arriving on the scene with already established upper classmen.

The director told us specifically not to watch or study the movie. *Too late!* I knew the part as it was in the movie and had no idea what making a part your own involved. Nevertheless, the role fit like a glove and I got wonderful reviews. I reveled in the process. My fellow students, professors, frat boys, and athletes were even noticing my performance. This was new territory for me. I even got to twirl a black cane in one of the musical numbers and Mr. Weaver, my history professor, noted in class that I had pointed my cane dangerously close to his face as I descended a ramp during the choreography. He was a good sport with a surprising sense of humor considering that all I knew of him were very, very long academic lectures.

We performed the musical in the former university cafeteria. Cleverly redesigned, the space had just the right feel for the notorious Kit Kat Club. My parents and my sister arrived in Jacksonville to attend a performance and I truly don't recall ever being nervous or apprehensive. That is, however, until that specific night and the New Year's Eve scene where the emcee appears as Father Time and then uncloaks to become Baby New Year. The audience always loved the gag and I could deliver it with audacious assurance. But of course on this night, the first time anyone from my family would see me in my element, it took a turn.

When the time came to reveal Baby New Year, I had a wardrobe malfunction. A really good wardrobe malfunction. My diaper fell at my feet.

Now I wasn't completely naked underneath, I had a tiny jock strap for a covering. My lower limbs were exposed like a lily-white pair of chicken legs. The audience roared to a volume level we had not heard before. My parents and my sister teased me about that moment for years to come. It really was hilarious and you know what? I didn't mind. The gag worked. Sometimes you go for it and you roll with the punches. Embrace those moments of embarrassment and stay in character. Again, I would own the mishap and embrace it.

The art of recovery is a requirement in any kind of performance. With the added distress of a high-flying piece of equipment or prop, we have to learn very quickly to cover the mistake and continue without anyone being distracted. Things can go wrong. Things will inevitably go amiss in big ways or in tiny gnat-like annoyances. Dancers slip, actors get tongue-tied, or a gymnast falls. Figure skaters lose an edge or a color guard person gets a flag caught in some outdated citation chord safety pinned to a shoulder (true story). We can miss a beat or a note. The art of recovery is a fact of life. We experience the loss of people we are certain we cannot live without. Heartache can seem unbearable. We either learn to embrace it or we stop right where we are with no forward momentum.

Momentum

CHAPTER 4

Experience

These days, with more commercial exposure and the Internet, I receive emails and messages from a lot of young people. I'm often asked about how to get started in the business or how to develop a career in the pageantry arts. They're interested in designing or teaching marching band, drum and bugle corps or color guard. They want to know how to pursue a variety of areas that might lead to commercial work, or special events like corporate conventions and halftime entertainment at bowl games. These are tough questions to answer and, in our world especially, there's no one way to success or easy route to follow. But I always start with two words: Get Experience. Now I'm a firm believer in there being exceptions to every rule, but this advice holds true through my own situation and certainly through our vast and ever-evolving history.

Tam was the first person to tell me that I should audition for the Madison Scouts Drum and Bugle Corps. It was a fantasy for me, but I had no idea what would be involved or if I was even ready. I equated everything to what little I knew about the entertainment worlds of theatre and film, so in my head The Madison Scouts represented the "Professionals" of the marching world even though, unfortunately, it is not a paid job. Later on, I would alter my presumption to consider performing with a top-level organization to getting your doctorate. It's the highest level of education a person can get when it comes to the pageantry art world without being financially compensated. We pay dues to be a part of the experience and we get top instruction from some of the best and brightest in the business.

While I was growing up, my parents had always provided us with a sense of safety and financial security. I didn't know we didn't have an awful lot of money and was shocked as an adult to discover the low level of pay my mother received for being a registered nurse. It would become another example of how our society undervalues the very people who shape the future or care for its inhabitants. When I called to ask if I could make the journey to Madison, Wisconsin to audition for this prestigious group, it was no wonder that my father responded with a resounding "NO." Without the details and information, my father could only assume that this would be costly and maybe an endeavor I was not prepared for.

I went anyway. Once again my impish disobedience thoughtlessly controlled my actions and I foolishly assumed I could keep it a secret. *Or did I really have a choice?*

The weekend was like Wonderland for me. This was a big audition and the numbers to me seemed staggering. An abundance of talent, all male, was passionate about performing with one of the world's top drum corps. The gymnasium was filled to capacity with guys auditioning simply for the color guard. Here I was, amid a diverse room full of talent, doing the very thing that seemed to me so natural. And let's clear something up right now: Not every guy who performs with color guard is gay. Through the years there are many ignorant and uninformed people who like to declare that assumption. Nothing is further from the truth. The importance of stating that fact is that here I was, among guys from varying backgrounds including straight AND gay, allowing me to exercise the very talent that so many had teased and taunted me for in the past. Here was a place, in 1978, where what mattered was doing your job.

I also met one of the best designers, teachers, and mentors I have ever known—Sylvester "Sal" Salas. Sal was in charge of the Madison Scout's Color Guard and also directed and designed an up and coming winter guard, The State Street Review. Sal had a championship background in his own right; he was, and still is, a true innovator who has influenced every aspect of the pageantry arts world. Sal is another one of many individuals who deserve more accolades than I could ever extol. He deserves every honor that he could possibly receive and has probably trained more successful students than any other designer/instructor in our long history. Hell, he's probably trained more students than anyone in color guard and continues today still offering his exceptional perspective and talents.

On Sunday, the last day of the camp, Sal called me into a tiny foyer outside the gym. He told me he wanted me to be a part of the rifle line. I had passed the audition. *Are you serious? Is this happening?* I like to think I glanced over my shoulder to see that elfish little boy with his broken baton, smiling with joy.

Now something really interesting happened. I immediately went to find a pay phone. Yes, a pay phone. I nervously dropped the quarter into the black box on the wall and made a collect call home to Georgia. My father answered the phone. I could picture him in the hall where our one phone sat on a fake wooden table, the receiver chord dangling at his side. I explained the situation and tried to be apologetic for my disobedience while obviously unable to hide my excitement. I finally got to the part where I could tell him that I had earned a spot.

My father paused then said.

"You made it? Well I guess you really wanna do this, huh?"

"Yes, sir." I replied.

I have no idea how the conversation proceeded after that moment. It was probably something about telling me to be careful and to call home as soon as I returned to Jacksonville.

Back at JSU my classes in dance and theatre continued. I was being introduced to great choreographers and their individualism. Names like Martha Graham, Merce Cunningham, and Twyla Tharp were becoming part of my newfound inspiration. I was a sponge. I performed with indoor competitive color guard for the first time with The Southern Lancers. On certain weekends through the winter months, those of us joining The Madison Scouts would travel to Wisconsin for camps in preparation for the summer.

A group of us traveled to Chicago, Illinois to the very first Winter Guard International Championship. Prior to this season a national competition did not exist during the winter months and circuits around the country crowned their own champions. I watched the entire preliminary competition from beginning to end. This enlightened gathering of top groups from around the country showcased diverse styles, approaches, and regional differences. It was electric and revealing. Suddenly the options were endless and creativity and innovation flourished in an indescribable way. Not only did this event bring together amazing talented performers, it also began to highlight some of the industries top designers, instructors and judges who, for me, were clearly celebrities. From brilliant creators like George Zingali, John Brasale, or Stanley Knaub, to judges like Donald Angelica, Shirlee Whitcomb, George Olivero, or Marie Czapinski, it was thrilling.

I loved every single performance, I was a "super fan," and I took copious notes in the program. Again, I was wide-eyed and eager to convince the world that they should be witnessing this extraordinary happening. And one performing ensemble in particular would bravely set the foundation for my own approach and development.

Mary Doolittle Burns, in her red ballet slippers, stood at the entrance to the competition floor with grace and confidence. The music of Respighi filled the space and onto the floor bounded the sprite-like whirlwind of energy known as The Seattle Imperials. To say that Stanley Knaub, their choreographer/director, was an innovator is an understatement. Stanley and The Seattle Imperials had already set out exploding the boundaries of color guard. Historically military based with occasional variations beyond marching styles and basic body positions, The Imperials offered a dimensionality and display of legitimate techniques that expanded the palate of motion. Rejected by traditionalist and idolized by others; their commitment to new ideas catapulted the possibility of musical interpretation. Stanley had created a tidal wave of an approach that would become what is now considered inherent. I knew from the moment they entered the floor that this philosophy was the map to my future. The wide-ranging pieces of my world existed simultaneously so why wouldn't the creative process include that collection of imaginative options. It was irrefutable to me that dance and color guard would coexist and Stanley had brought this idea into reality.

Stanley knew what so many people understood in a post modern dance world. Everything is dance. With The Seattle Imperials, he tossed aside the military boots for ballet slippers, all the while maintaining the excellence and entertainment values of our history.

The actress Beverly D'Angelo tells a story (which I'm sure I can't replicate with accuracy) about auditioning for the movie version of the musical *Hair*. Twyla Tharp was set to choreograph and Beverly D'Angelo was apprehensive about her ability to handle the dance that would be involved. She went for an audition with Twyla Tharp and expressed her concerns and anxiety.

Twyla told her, "Dance is anything that can be repeated twice."

Twyla had her run across the room. Then she told her to do it again in the same manner. Beverly complied even including gestures that she had previously and naturally performed.

Twyla responded, "See, you're dancing."

I love the idea that we are all dancing our way through life and its multifarious everyday motions. I appreciate the thought of everyone enjoying the liberating release of dance. I've never understood the resistance to this natural human act of physicality enhancing the worlds of color guard, drum and bugle corps, or marching band. It made perfect sense to me.

Stanley brought the legitimate world of dance to color guard, drum corps, and marching band. When you see the incredible musicians moving dimensionally through programs involving true technique and skill, it's because of Stanley. When you see the leaps and bounds of grace, athleticism, and expressiveness through today's color guards and drum corps, it's because of Stanley. When you witness the power and dynamics of physical beauty through the ever-evolving world of drum and bugle corps it is because of Stanley. Stanley Knaub made it real. And because he demanded, through technical and expressive training, that performers communicate at the highest levels, we owe him everything. Stanley encouraged innovation and exuded intensity. I still use Stanley's techniques to this day and I am a firm believer in his use of breath as a means to unify pre-show concentration. He lived his strong opinions. He was my mentor, my teacher, my cheerleader, and my friend. And most of all he encouraged me to honor who I uniquely could be.

And now a story about gawking…

Although I had seen drum and bugle corps on television, instructional videos, and old performance movies, I had never seen a drum corps show live in person. It's hard to believe that the first live drum corps performance I witnessed was from the football field as a performer with The Madison Scouts. Off the field I was a bug-eyed "kid in a candy store." I was ecstatic and took every opportunity to watch every moment that I could of the other competitors. This was a chance to see in person the newsprint photos I had clipped from the few drum corps tabloids available.

Each competition was an exciting new chance to see a group I hadn't seen before. One night, fresh from the field and sweat drenched after our performance, the Scouts began to circle up for comments and announcements. It's a chance for the staff to exercise their coaching prowess and the commentary always let us know how the overall performance had unfolded. I, however, got sidetracked peering through the chain link fence at the drum corps performance immediately following us. Mesmerized and entranced, I was unaware of the required gathering behind me; I couldn't take my eyes off the performance happening on the field.

Suddenly I felt a strong hand on my neck. A veteran member of The Scouts abruptly turned me around and I was shocked into reality. It was Todd Ryan. As an older member of the corps, Todd was in a leadership position and quickly let me know that I was supposed to be with "our" corps and not gawking at the one on the field. It was all a very silent movie, complete with black screen subtitles, and the rattle of old timey piano. I mugged submission.

Now here's the really fun part. The drum and bugle corps on the field that had so enthralled me in my helpless fascination was none other than The Blue Devils from Concord, California. Years later Todd Ryan and I would both end up working with this amazing organization.

Drum Corps, which are non-profit organizations, tour the country during the summer months housed in high school or college gymnasiums, sometimes even dormitories or, on very special occasions, hotels. American Drum Corps have even taken special excursions to compete, perform in exhibitions or parades, and sometimes conduct clinics in other countries. Drum Corps tours with the summer heat and a hectic travel schedule can often be demanding and taxing. In my youth I didn't mind the exhausting schedule or the accommodations so much. I was amazed, with an all male group in particular, that this assortment of testosterone could maturely navigate the long hours, cramped quarters, un-air-conditioned buses or public showers. It didn't matter whom you were, veteran or rookie, straight or gay, rich or poor, you were there to do a job. That sense of discipline and team mentality appealed to me.

No matter what your pursuit, there's no accounting for experiencing the process and the endless hours of work involved. It's impossible to fabricate the physical awareness, the tension and the nerves, or the moments where laughter and shenanigans shake the strained atmosphere into relaxed submission. The ability to live in close proximity with any number of people and feel that sense of collaborative cohesion is invaluable. You learn to handle the days when you'd love to be anywhere else and especially enjoy a spot of privacy. You learn your coworker's mood swings, emotional hot buttons, and often what can ease a delicate moment. You learn how to hold up your end of the performance no matter how you may feel. You learn how to trust your training and have faith in your technique.

It's all show business even though it's referred to as a "youth" activity. There's an audience who has paid good money to come and see you and you have something to communicate. But you also quickly become aware that before you know it, in the blink of an eye, what you are spending all this time on will soon be a memory. The stadium or the arena or the theatre will be empty and the lights will be turned off. You'll move on to the next show, the next job, or the next phase of your life. All for the better, because you have experienced something tangible, meaningful, and real.

CHAPTER 5

Blessings in Disguise

The Southern Lancers indoor color guard upgraded to become a winter guard called Chapter Five. The name came from the fact that it was the fifth year for this pursuit and many of the same people were involved from the previous years. It was a stylistic change, a fun show, and allowed a few of us to perform and create the show at the same time. It also allowed me to exercise my solo chops during the show that gave me another one of those magic moments that people recognized and remind me of to this day. We made the finals at the 1979 Championships for WGI and the experience was successful without me having any memory of placement or scores. That year I also got to meet Stanley Knaub and years later, working and creating together, we would laugh about how I behaved in such a state of star-struck mania that Stanley even thought it was a little creepy. I was speechless and examining Stanley as if he were some sort of sorcerer. Stanley would later dub me "The Pixie from Dixie" and laughed often about our first meeting.

At the same time so many delightful things were happening for me, I was dealing with insecurities, for whatever reason, and dealing with the guilt that I might be wasting my parent's money. I was just barely starting to grasp the concept of finances. When my father informed that he would be selling the trombone I was no longer playing to help with bills, it all started to become clear that proceeding on my parent's dime, in whatever crazy direction I might be drawn, was simply not possible, or fair. I was even holding down part-time work, but still unable to make ends meet. I can have all the best intentions, but my self-sabotage ensues and I can't say I was always responsible or resourceful.

My plans were to continue in Madison until I hit a stress-riddled, guilt-paneled wall that pretty much made the decision for me. I needed to get a job. I needed money. These days we work hard to provide potential performers with sponsorship information or scholarship programs. But here I was, feeling inadequate at problem solving; guilty for the financial burden I was placing on others, and regretful for leaving my fellow performers. I would have to forget about a second year of drum corps (for now). I was fortunate to find an option that would allow me to still pursue my color guard aspirations and maybe become a little more responsible. I headed to Dallas, Texas and Marching Auxiliaries of America.

Marching Auxiliaries of America or "M.A." is a dynamic company that started as the brainchild of Mike Mastandrea and Donna Haas. Providing training for auxiliary groups including Drum majors, majorettes, feature twirlers, color guards, drill and dance teams, M.A. would run a series of instructional camps throughout the country. What started as a passion project for this inspiring couple soon progressed to one of the nation's leaders in an industry that offered incredible alternatives to those schools, teams, and groups that didn't necessarily have an in-house staff. Marching Auxiliaries even branched out to exciting performance opportunities with college bowl games, and international travel including The World's Fair in Seville, Spain. They have continued to expand the company to include competitions and private camps. The wonderful attributes that make up M.A. can all be traced to the intensely professional and lively personalities of Mike and Donna.

Once again I would be surrounded by astonishingly talented people and learn to incorporate new ideas, techniques, and styles into my ever-expanding imagination. The exposure to dance and drill team would especially influence my approach and the idea of artfulness mixed with precision movement would astound me. Mike and Donna were quick to recruit staff and performers who were current, contemporary, and well versed in the innovative ideas of the day. I was suddenly in a whirlwind of talent from legendary places such as The Kilgore Rangerettes. I was a super fan. I was observing the mastery of people including Bruce Hart, a former drum major from Ohio State University. There were award-winning twirlers and dancers with experience in New York or Los Angeles. There were highly intelligent, incredibly hilarious, creative people. It was a remarkable opportunity and another chance to feel accomplished and home.

Furthermore, I was teaching enthusiastic students every day and creatively learning to incorporate their individual talents and skills into routines and choreography. The students came in all shapes and sizes, and with varying levels of experience and backgrounds so learning to think quickly in the moment became essential. I loved the menagerie of personalities. Communication became key when discovering ways to offer information and make it an enjoyable experience. I studied closely the manner in which Mike and Donna handled themselves professionally. They were amazingly business like and personable when dealing with clients, students or staff. Mike would pace the floor while talking on the phone, harnessing the energy that I instantly felt in his presence. Donna could offer the information or instruction I needed directly and succinctly, the entire time making me feel comfortable and confident.

Each week the camps would end with an evaluation that allowed the campers to earn ribbons and awards. I enjoyed crafting and stylizing the routines so that the "bug" of performance could bite these young performers. I could take what were stock routines taught to "off the shelf" band music and tailor make them to fit the talent in front of me. I loved it. And I loved that these wide-eyed innocents could be thrilled by the moment. I also felt like an ambassador for movement and color guard, still reeling with images of The Seattle Imperials in my head. Mike and Donna allowed me to show WGI videos of winter guards to the campers. I would gab on and on about the various groups, styles, and people I thought of as superstars. I'm not kidding about being a guard geek at all. Remember, I attended the very first WGI Championships and took extensive notes in my program. I'd covered the photos and copy in the first program with my reverential musings.

I developed a special bond with Donna. If she approved of me, or my work, my self-esteem grew and I flourished. If Donna had a criticism, I took it to heart and diligently worked to make the appropriate corrections. She had twirled baton and danced, and was generous with technical and expressive lessons. She was a caring person, like so many of the brilliant teachers I have known, who can offer the positive or the negative in a way that allowed me to feel safe to embrace it because it comes with unconditional love. She could also call out my less than stellar moments. Donna likes to refer to me as the "number one son." I idolized her and still do to this day. Throughout the years she has never wavered in her support for who I am and what I do. She always had a sense of when I needed to move on or when my frenetic energy needed focus.

She's a bright and shining star to me.

And now a story about the fast and the curious…

There were a few early years where Marching Auxiliaries held a training week for staff at Nichols State University in Thibodaux, Louisiana. The sizable, diverse staff from all the different specialty areas of auxiliaries would gather to organize routines, techniques, and a demonstration performance. It was all in preparation for the extensive calendar of summer clinics. It was lively, fun, fast, and exciting and I might add, humid. But it was great to have dorms, the university facilities and the proximity to New Orleans. I was sponging up material from all the talent. I would learn baton tricks. I would beg the Rangerettes to teach me choreography. And I would spend every moment I could with Donna and Susan Stevens Crummel, the brilliant children's book author. Susan was another one of those wonderful people who had a background in pageantry, understood the importance of arts education in schools, and showed a deep respect for even the greenest of newbies like me. I absorbed every second I could of them talking shop and tried to make them laugh as much as possible.

On one of those cinematic Louisiana nights, Donna asked Bruce Hart and I to accompany her to the airport to fetch Brenda Collins. Brenda was feature twirler at the University of Kentucky, an expert instructor, and hilarious. I'm not kidding, she was smart and funny—she was my Lily Tomlin. Everything went smoothly until the trip back to the university from the New Orleans airport.

Now the route to the school was on back roads just like you would imagine, this being nighttime, humid, hot, sticky, dusty, graveled, frog-serenaded, deep-in-the-South Louisiana. Add to that my vivid imagination and you'll understand my proclivity to exaggerate. Either the biblical rapture had occurred or everyone was nestled away fast asleep in their homes. It was dark and virtually desolate as we made our way through small towns on our way back. And we were in a rental van full of leftover belongings that so many of the staff members had yet to retrieve. Old magazines, various pieces of clothing, shoes, and a few bags of fast food trash that surprisingly had accumulated on the short drive from Dallas for some of us.

Donna was driving and Brenda was in the passenger seat. The next seat back was Bruce, and I was laid out in the very backseat of the van. We came to a red light in a small town that felt like the middle of nowhere. And, I don't know how, but there was suddenly a pickup truck behind us. It was probably a perfectly respectable pickup truck, but in my mind it was gross, rusty, and probably had the words, "I will kill u" spray-painted on the hood. It's all fodder for any B-movie horror flick. You get the picture. You can imagine me peering my little head out the back window fighting back the urge to pee on the seat.

For some unknown reason, what I think was the biggest redneck I have ever seen got out of that truck and walked up to the driver's window of the van. He was trying to talk to Donna for some mysterious reason and no; it was not a plea for help. He was belligerent. This guy reeked of "no-goodery." He may have even been the mayor of "no goodsville." I'm sure alcohol was involved. The light changed and Donna's instincts kicked in and by that I mean she put pedal to the metal. As we peeled out he hit the back of the van with his fist. Suddenly the soundtrack to every chase scene in every bad movie began to play in my head.

He and his partner in the truck began a game of cat and mouse with us for I don't know how long. They would tailgate us, pass us, back off just enough to make us think it was over, then start all over again. Donna was brilliant. She was racecar brilliant. I would learn that not only was Donna intelligent, beautiful, and talented—the girl could drive. She was controlling her own anxiety and masterfully accommodating the craziness. Now mind you, I'm flipping the f*&% out! In my head I was trying to jump ahead in the script and figure how Bruce and I were going to fight these two Neanderthals—as if Donna, after showcasing her raceway prowess, would ever need some sort of chivalrous defense from us. Regardless, I assumed I had better be prepared.

The chase was heating up when the truck began to pull up and swerve to force us off the road. Finally Donna had no choice but to veer off onto the gravel shoulder. She controlled the moment skillfully and we came to a stop with nothing more than a cloud of dust in the muggy darkness. This was it. Bruce and I would have to get out of the van and face the confrontation. Due to the fact that I had been lounging in the back seat until the unfortunate incident, I had no shoes on. I fumbled in the darkness of the back of the van, grappling at the floor. For some reason the only shoes I could find were…wait for it…pumps. High heels. My hyper imagination began to fast forward once again. *How on earth was I going be in a fight with these two obviously large, inebriated troglodytes while wearing heels? Is this really happening? Will these even fit me? Are they strapless? Can I run in gravel?*

Perhaps with the help of some guardian angel or a twist of fate, the pickup truck never stopped. The taillights of the monster faded into the night. We were safe. We didn't see them again and made it back to the university in one piece except for our frazzled nerves and a larger-than-life story. Everyone was amused at my comical, buffoonery amid all the drama. But not one person ever pointed out the obvious skew of my back-of-the-van activity. That is, until recently, all these years later, when I told the story to Karl Lowe.

Karl with his quick wit and super intelligence brought to my attention a most humiliatingly hilarious spin to my actions. In my tiny part of the story, I had not once entertained the thought of using the high heels as a weapon.

I had only thought of wearing them! Go figure.

Let's get back to Marching Auxiliaries. Donna and Mike also treated what we did as equal to any other professional endeavor. It's a philosophy that somehow was an inherent part of me since the very beginning. Remember, for me as a child, I looked at those teenagers in the high school marching band just like the celebrities and stars I saw on television or in magazines. Through the years I found it difficult to differentiate between one medium to another, one act of performance to the next, or the talented creators that inhabited those varied, exciting worlds. I held a romantic view of art in general and loosened the grips of definitions that might limit its opportunities. The idea that the pageantry arts are not "less than" anything else in the world sets a standard for me and informs everything I do to this day. Granted I realistically understand how society in general defines success. But if there is a question of the glass being half empty or half full—I want to create a new glass.

I would continue for two summers and even spent time helping out with two drum corps until the question of continuing at JSU prompted me to venture down uncertain roads. I have always regretted unfinished business, but something was pulling me and to where I had no idea. During my second summer I was spending time contributing to The Schaumburg Guardsmen. With their honored history and Bill Harty's belief in innovation, The Guardsmen were a rewarding experience. But it would be during this time that I began to get a clue. Plain and simple, I did not know enough. It was time to snap the rubber band of whimsy back into some sort of focus. I sought out Sal Salas during the end of that drum corps summer. I was honest and upfront with Sal and expressed my desire to get back to Madison and finish what I had started. It was an important admission. I begged. Learning how to acknowledge what I don't know is just as important as having faith in what I do know.

Sal was kind, caring, and understanding. So my plans were set to return to Madison, Wisconsin for the winter guard season and my final drum corps summer. Now don't think for a second that I suddenly had my act totally together. I could still be irresponsible, overly enthusiastic, and naïve—but there was a sense that I was making some headway in my quest towards maturity. I stumbled and faltered a few times and Sal and his wife, LuAnn were luckily there to save me. I would still find myself as Blanche Dubois, depending on the kindness of (not so) strangers. I was improving though, and had certainly grown, personally and creatively, from my time with Marching Auxiliaries. Sal, along with Tam and Mike Turner joining the staff, taking notice of my development, skills and confidence, saw fit to place me in a leadership role for the upcoming summer. I would be captain of The Madison Scouts color guard. *Imagine that! What would that teenager back in Georgia glued to the DCI broadcast on television think of this? Are they sure about this? Do they have any idea that on the inside I am riding way past the speed limit?*

I exercised discipline and followed instructions. The professionalism I had studied so closely with Mike and Donna was paying off for me. I made lifelong friends through the winter and summer and again reached a high point of experience regardless of scores or competitive results. Marlieta Matthews Beckman became one of the best friends I've ever known and we would huddle together on the rides to the winter competitions, gathering our courage and relishing in the performances. Marlieta had the same views I did when it came to this obscure activity where we resided. We could feel like "stars" with the State Street Review and cherish the positive response from audiences and fill our time with hard work and laughter. What we were doing mattered, and was important even if only to one single young admirer waiting for us when we exited the bus for a show.

Mike Turner had taken Stanley Knaub's lead and was diligently pursuing dance study. His classes and instruction helped shape a unique approach for The Madison Scouts that summer and movement was becoming more and more prevalent in color guard. Tam had become a mentor and teacher for me. And Sal was, well, the grand master. I liked to call Sal "Cecil B. DeMille," all grandiose and spectacle, creating character-driven productions that were unmatched. Sal also has a real knack for knowing just the right moment to insert the joke. It's a valuable lesson.

FWD March

And now a story about Rockford, Illinois…

The State Street Review winter color guard arrived in Rockford for a competition hosted by The Phantom Regiment. Stylishly dressed in street wear for the bus ride, State Street always had an aura about them and this show was no different than any other. Competition time rolled around and we continued our preparations as usual: dress in costume, warm up, and perform. We certainly wanted to win, but winning took a back seat to simply performing the show correctly and perfectly. *Now there's a lesson I have never forgotten.* We were maybe a minute into our performance when the dreaded sound problem occurred. The music completely cut out. We froze. *What happened? Are we done? Is that it? Was it a problem with the recording, the speakers, or the sound system?* We exited the gymnasium and circled up in an empty hallway. Sal informed us that there was a sound system problem and that we had a second to collect ourselves before we would return and start the performance over again. We were nervous. Tension surrounded us and we could hear the audience buzzing back inside the gymnasium. We were quickly losing our focus. Sal's quick wit kicked into gear and he started a humorous little chant to set us in motion back to the competition floor.

"Lions and tigers and bears, oh my!"

"Lions and tigers and bears, oh my!"

Everyone caught onto Sal's whispered chant and the rhythm quickly began to pull us all back together. The chant grew in volume and we became an adrenaline-fueled bundle of animation. He had, in a split second, found a way to ease the tension and make us act as one cohesive unit. We were trained, and we certainly trusted Sal, so this simply became a moment and memory that led us in our return to the floor; this time without any technical sound issues. Once again, I have no recollection of the competitive results that day, but I will never forget "Lions and tigers and bears, oh my!" and the ability to pull an ensemble back into collective focus. How you handle any level of crisis can define you and move you forward or bring you to complete halt. That day we moved forward.

CHAPTER 6

Live/Play/Live

Drum Corps International and Winter Guard International both had an age limit for competitors at this time. WGI has since lifted their age limitations in certain divisions. In 1981 it would be my time to no longer compete in both venues. I was an "age-out." Often being an age-out marks a time of moving on and leaving the youthful experience behind. People always like to say it's a time to "get on with your life." So here I was entertaining the myriad possibilities and continuing to believe I could do more than one thing. I was like one of the Great Lakes filled with only a foot of water—I only knew a little, but aspired to a lot.

He may have been a controversial man, but Donald Angelica was one of the greatest chief judges of Drum Corps International. Unquestionably educated, Donald had an appetite for culture and remained current on music, theatre, and fine art. He was an educator, a politician, iconic, intensely decisive, and wore his power like couture. His eccentricity and opinionated ideals guided much of the innovation that drum corps and marching band have become today. He also had an eye for spotting talent and didn't mind playing agent to various assortments of collaboration. Those of us that Donald maneuvered through circumstances could often feel like chess pieces in some sophisticated game—but more often than not, Donald was right. Every conversation with Donald was a lesson. He also commandeered my move to New York City and proof that drum corps can continue to be an education far beyond your performing years. I would soon be studying dance in Manhattan and teaching at an entry level among legends of our activity.

Something astounding was happening at The Garfield Cadets during this time. A spirit of innovation and an enthusiastic barrier breaking energy was distilling through the efforts of talented people including George Zingali, Jim Prime, Michael Cesario, and Greg Cesario. I had basically been drafted to come aboard to teach the rifle line. My rides to rehearsal with Sue Erban were full of history lessons on this New Jersey iconic drum corps. It would be a few months of watching this magical time unfold before Donald invited me to dinner for what sounded like a serious discussion.

Down the way a bit from Garfield is Bayonne, New Jersey—home to the Bayonne Bridgemen. In the city the contrast between the jazz-fueled Latin-tinged movement of Phil Black and the Graham expounded May O'Donnell Dance Centre where I was taking classes was also apparent in the two drum corps I was straddling. If Garfield was evolving into a museum of fine art, then the Bridgemen were all grease paint and smoky stage doors. The Bridgemen had an opening for someone to lead their color guard. We sat at dinner and Donald told me why this would be the opportunity I needed to keep moving forward. It wouldn't be long before Bobby Hoffman, grand master of the Bridgemen, joined us at the restaurant. I had long been a fan of the Bridgemen and their no-nonsense appeal and unabashed sense of humor. There was something quite rebellious in the face of traditional drum corps philosophy that they brought to performances. Albeit highly entertaining, they could still provide a commentary on how stifling the institution of drum corps could be. Not only that, but my mother had taken a liking to them and knowing she would be amused helped me make up my mind. I went to work with the Bayonne Bridgemen.

In 1983 after DCI had brought in famed choreographer Pat Birch to provide television commentary, she would tell me how much she appreciated the sense of "street smart" that the Bridgemen's choreography brought to the event. There among the military foundations were the bawdy, unapologetic Bridgemen and ultimately I would be thankful I had taken the job even though the competitive accolades were destined for The Garfield Cadets. Not only would I be surrounded by an energetic and challenging staff, but a personality-driven color guard full of overwhelming talent and perseverance and one of the greatest drum lines DCI has known. Dennis DeLucia, percussion caption head, was proof that amid the eccentric entertainment of a super stylized corps that competitive excellence could coexist. I was exposed to the musicianship and professionalism of Grammy-award winner Frank Dorritte who one day stumbled upon me playing his music score on the piano. Broadway dancer Rob Draper came in to set the 1982 tap dance on the tables and encouraged me to interject myself more into the choreography. It was an exciting time. I still cherish those color guard performers and the staff there for fostering a newbie and ultimately, Bobby Hoffman who just kept encouraging me to be as creative and inventive as possible. There would be two ever present requirements at hand: it should be fun and you have to play.

There are all kinds of people involved in what we do. Personalities run the gamut of a color wheel with shades of jeweled depth to shocking neon: all filling the hours with a constant maze of emotions. Everyone wants your ability and your talent, and your ideas become a commodity. But most of all, I think even in the most professional of situations; everyone wants someone that can blend the work with a sense of fun. No one wants to be pulled down, or constantly walking on eggshells or residing in a state of avoidance. Most people, sans the power-driven egomaniacal, want someone who makes everyone look better. I was learning the fine balance between the sense of work ethic and the ability to play. It started from the beginning for me and continues to this day. There is a time and a place for every mood swing and often, especially for me in the creative process, freedom is key. It's all about getting the job done (and done well), but ultimately, we want to feel secure throughout the creative mine field we negotiate. For me it always depends on the task at hand. But that sense of work and play was always evident with Mickey Kelley and The Skylarks winter color guard from Connecticut. Mickey, a master of pacing and detail, could shift from a "problem solving" instant to an outbreak of comedy with a single sentence.

The Skylarks competitive color guard possessed indisputable style. It was a unique brand that I had observed through the years at WGI. They could shift from pulsing disco to "Steam Heat" to patriotic salutes with agility and brilliant musicality. Every season could be entirely different from the previous one and yet they were instantly recognizable. Jeff Namian had been with The Skylarks for a few years before I was East-Coast bound. We had been a part of The Madison machine together and he wanted me to meet Mickey and it didn't take long to feel at home with The Skylarks. Once again I would have the chance to gain experience while acting in a small role. It was pressure-free and full of grand personalities. I loved it and I loved watching everyone work there: brand new lessons and joyful experiences. We worked hard and we laughed a lot. Jeff and I were notorious for chuckling from the sidelines, amused with endless fits of silliness. Even to the point of Mickey ordering us from the rehearsal, we'd quickly collect ourselves and return to the task at hand. We were young; full of ideas and Mickey was perfect at not only tolerating us, but also at developing our skills.

I was just starting out and working for little to no money and I considered these years like an internship. Unable to ask for more than the chance to learn and participate in the process, I would appreciate this period knowing that there would be time enough later for shouldering the bulk of responsibility. I remember clearly being aware of the stress-laden pressure that those who lead the process must endure. That level of accountability to the performers, to the audiences, and to our history is not taken lightly.

OK, so we weren't rocket science or brain surgery, but our small world of entertainment and competition could be a serious game of expression and communication. Young performers would be gaining life experience in competition, collaboration, and endurance, but it was a creative endeavor, which became license to laugh for me. And the sense of "play" would keep the mind clear enough to let new ideas emerge. I still find it difficult to downplay or disregard what we do, but I'm sensitive to the need to break the tension or the monotony of any moment.

Well then now might be a good time. Should I tell everyone about my stint as a universal sign model? You might know me from my "cross the street now" pose, or my "men's room" man on door. OK, get back to it.

FWD March

I was in love with the 1986 Spirit of Atlanta color guard. I started there in 1984, and by 1986 the color guard had amassed an incredible amount of talent that was literally growing up with the program. By the summer of '86 with Tam acting as program coordinator and Sal writing the drill, I was basically handling the bulk of writing for the color guard. Infused with an eclectic assortment of styles and techniques, we ran the gamut from my admiration for Fosse to the result of technique I was studying with a former Ailey dancer in Atlanta. In my head, as usual, the fantasy of a contemporary ensemble being relevant to current culture was imperative. And the drive to produce something that could stand alongside any popular entertainment form burned the process with passion and style. I was always lost inside that professional, multimillion-dollar pretend world of escape—all the time operating on a small budget and enormous aspirations. This particular group of male and female performers was a cohesive fusion of skill, style, and larger-than-life personality. It honestly seemed like we were magically in the same place at the same time with a flair for bringing this southern drum corps persona to fruition.

The choreographic process was a natural progression that probably for the first time for me seemed more like improvisational recreation than laboriously over studied. I was choreographing so specifically to the performers and their unique *je ne sais quoi* that the time never felt regulated or excessively scheduled. The learning process was a playful, "follow me" kind of exercise with music blasting from a worn cassette or fits of silly characterization. The entire summer seemed like a cyclonic whirl of intense sessions of sweating followed by games of Hacky Sack. It resonated through their performances and we almost won our second DCI guard title that summer. Style and substance were evenly matched and completely in sync. To the outsider, and perhaps the performers themselves, it may have seemed like more goofball antics than grueling hours of exertion, but no one gets that good without training, skill, perseverance, and hard work. I'm glad that the performers might recall the fun first and foremost. For me, this color guard set a standard that summer.

Years later I would venture to Boston to create some work for another winter color guard—St. Ann's. As so many Boston color guards do, they had a reputation for high-level equipment training. The methods, skills, and expert comfort that they exhibited when manipulating rifles and sabers or flags were precise and autonomous. I went through my usual paces freeing my mind up to simply reflect and rely on the music to speak. That particular year they were ending the performance with all the performers on rifles. It was exciting, but also risky if any individual faltered. It was the last impression for the audience and the judges; the music was powerful and as daring as the situation. This would not be a time for subtlety. I worked with my back to them improvising through the music for quite a bit of time thinking that eventually I would turn around to explain the choreography in detail. I was playing out the fantasy in my head like I always do, imagining myself in the packed arena or as a character in some cinematic reel. I had spent time observing them and working on other parts and this gave me internal information that hopefully provided me with a basis to design specifically for this group of people. Here's the kicker—when I felt as though my rough draft was complete enough to begin the explanation process, they had been following the entire time and knew the phrase. Their training had allowed them to follow my improvised moment and sure, it wasn't all detailed yet, but they understood the arc of the moment from beginning to end. I was amazed and impressed. There was no barking of orders and instructions, no rapid fire interrupting corrections. It was a moment of them and me…simply playing.

That sense of play allows everyone to release tension and I don't mind being silly at all in front of the performers. As long as I'm progressing forward and inching closer to the goal, the freedom to explore can be liberating and surprisingly beneficial in a multitude of ways. There are times when I have planned it all out and other times when I'm purely letting myself react to the bigger ideals of the moment. Discovery is just that—a time to learn what never before seemed imaginable. And it can be joyful and fun.

Jay Murphy is a big proponent of design by discovery. With a rich history in all areas of pageantry, Jay is incredibly intelligent and has instincts that are fine-tuned and exceedingly accurate. He demands spontaneity and authenticity and the results are always living, breathing, dynamic performance vehicles of staging. I've come to realize that Jay's process of staging or creating drill "in the moment" or "on the spot" is actually preceded by hours of painstaking thought and familiarity with music, theme, and concepts. And yet, this impulse driven process is in itself a form of play. With his work for the competitive winter guard the San Jose Raiders and the Blue Devils Drum and Bugle Corps and winter guard, I've witnessed first hand Jay's need to work in 3D. The regimental charts and geometric blueprints often used for learning staging or form became a limitation.

In 2013 with *The Re:Rite of Spring* we would have no charts of drum corps drill, only painstakingly sculpted multi-dimensional forms that, like choreography, had to be totally realized and morphed through spontaneity during the live performance. Now that essence of "play" would spring from the process to the live performance requiring the musicians and color guard to be in an active state of high alert throughout each show. The performers would no longer solely have individual coordinates or "dots" that allowed them to cocoon themselves in their own individual mathematic position. There would be certain sets meticulously charted, but there was no complete set of drill pages, no drill book if you will, as the past had dictated. It was eleven and a half minutes of 150 performers remaining sensitive to one another with every breath and every step. This was an evolution of years of discovery and not necessarily right for every type of presentation, but it would reveal a fresh potential for design and performance.

And now a story about being on the road for much too long…

Touring means a lot of time riding on long stretches of road with not much to do other than fill the time with equally long stretches of conversation and delirium. One of the best of those running conversations occurred one summer with Jay. For some reason we had embarked on a conversation about how we grew up watching television shows and cartoons where the animals could talk, act, and think like humans, One thing led to another until we stumbled upon an imaginary world of animal drum corps. Maybe you've all played this game before, but in the moment we couldn't get enough. It lasted for a few days. It was a drum corps version of *Animalympics*. Remember that show with its animated animals participating in a variety of sports? It was one of a long history of cartoons with animals doing human things.

Thus came our exploration of the species and their amusing or torrid drum corps activities. There are varying levels of funny, but you'll get the idea. The animal kingdom was not necessarily handling the drum corps competition with grace. There had, within the creature realm been controversy after controversy. One of the most famous stories was the yearly disqualification of the rabbits. It seems they would start their performance well within the limit of performing members, but easily double their size half way through their allotted performance time. Year after year, warning after warning, the rabbits had to endure the fate of disqualification. It was legendary.

The audience at these events could also suffer confusion and bewilderment. It seems they were forced to stare at a completely vacant field of nothingness while the Chameleons were competing.

The warm-up area could be a Darwinesque dangerous place. In an alarming fury, the timing and penalty judge, followed by the show sponsors frantically searched for the Canaries. That is, until they found the Cats brass line warming up; tiny yellow feathers exited the bells of their horns and rode the air like miniscule gondolas to the ground.

Competition could be nerve-racking and downright petrifying. The Deer were fine until the first reaction from the audience. It made for a great photograph though.

Year after year, everyone knew exactly what was going to happen with the Kangaroos. "What, something's coming out of that pouch? What a surprise."

There was also controversy when groups could be charged with having an unfair advantage: The Octopus.

The Pythons denied any wrongdoing, but the evidence was clear when we could see the silhouettes of the Meerkats in their midsections.

It felt like the Tortoises were on the field FOREVER!

FWD March

CHAPTER 7

Applause, A-pause

I wish I cared less about what people think. We create to communicate and I'm sure, for better or for worse, that I carry residual angst from a less than ordinary childhood. Anyone, no matter what the medium, yearns to speak and to be heard. Not only to be heard, but to be truly understood. It takes courage. It takes risking the rejection, vitriolic reactions, or worse yet, the disregard that carries no consideration whatsoever. Audience apathy is painful. Experiences with audiences can run the gamut from standing ovation to deafening silence. Audiences can be entranced or incensed. My own personal need for approval starts with the performers. I create for performers to showcase their talents and enjoy a fresh experience. And I certainly hope that the performers can build a relationship with their audience. But this does not exclude my sincere hope that the audience won't punish the performers because of my part in the process. Unfortunately the fact that I won't pander to an audience comes with a price. There will always be some people who just don't like what you do.

I respect the audience. They pay their hard-earned money to come and enjoy performances, take part in the sport of competition, and support the "teams" they love. Some people enjoy the nostalgia of a time when they participated in the arts. Family, friends, students, teachers, lovers of music, of motion, of color—the list of who might be sitting in the audience at any given performance is endless. They are as varied as the population of the world. People with different backgrounds and different professions make up a diverse collection of personal experiences which on any given day or night can result in feeling sad, or excited, or hungry or tired.

Years ago I would begin to understand that although I always want to make the audience happy, I would never insult them by pretending that I knew exactly what they wanted. And I can honestly say that I've never intentionally set out to displease them. A renowned chef once spoke to the fact that he never cooked for his customers. *Gasp.* His respect for his patrons would never allow him to be so presumptuous as to predict their palate at any given moment in time. He would simply create dishes and offer them with humility. It is quite often the reason why the discussion of "entertainment" perplexes me. I could never exercise the arrogance to define for others what may or may not be entertaining for them. And there is certainly no guaranteed formula for what is entertaining. Even members of the audience don't always agree on what is or is not entertaining. Entertainment is a spectrum of circumstances that is influenced by numerable factors that will forever be a topic of discussion.

Even though my first priority is the performers, I spend a lot of time observing the audience. At shows and competitions from Murfreesboro, TN to San Antonio, TX to Riverside, CA I often make my way through the crowds eavesdropping on their comments and opinions. Each and every audience is different. I have overheard the best and the worst—all of which has always been informative. I have been stopped and thanked, or have inched my way from the ridicule of a pointing finger. I've received letters and emails that ranged from joyful to downright hateful. My favorite comments come from children. Unfettered and insightful in their simplicity, they can strip the most complex and intellectually designed program down to its barest of essentials. They innately understand the visceral and the indefinable. Their reactions are not woven with nostalgia or history. And, quite courageously, children do not succumb to the collective conscience of audiences engulfed in competitive desire. I have listened to children comment on the mirrors from the Blue Devils 2010 program as "trippy" or the 2013 *Re:Rite of Spring* as "awesome." Their investment is quite different from adults and one that I often heed diligently.

Thanks to Beth Karlin I had begun in 1997 working at James Logan High School from Union City, California with the marching band and color guard programs. I had long been an admirer of these remarkable students and their ability to connect with the audience. The incredible talent and their ineffable spark were evident even when Scott Pizani began the indoor competitive program. Their rapport with the audience was astounding, and the only credit I could take for this was in providing a vehicle for the inevitable to happen. I would simply put them all in the same room and allow the chemistry to materialize. I offered some diverse settings for this to occur ranging from classical to pop to experimental. The expert technical staff devised a concrete foundation that, once ingrained, could allow the performers to literally live in the moment, "play" if you will, and this duality of concentration was impressive.

After a nod to the millennium featuring a complex soundtrack at the WGI 2000 Championship, I decided it would be fun to see the Logan aesthetic applied to a well-known and often used piece of music. *Carmina Burana* with its well-known melody of "O Fortuna" would be the basis for *Immortal Captive*. Linking shapes of bodies embossed on the floor formed the wheel of fate, and the narrative explored the never-ending cyclical journey we all take through life and ultimately must confront. It's typical that I prefer shows that work on multiple levels allowing the viewer to either enjoy the ride at face value or read into it and experience the motivation behind what could hopefully provide a "light bulb" moment.

The audience and our fellow competitors were so kind and supportive after their Championship finals performance that it brought me to tears. They exited the floor not only to the adulation of the spectators, but also to the resounding applause and smiling faces of their peers. It was a rare moment.

As much as we can think that every single individual in the audience enjoys our work, it's never the case. Imagine asking every single person to state his or her favorite food, or his or her favorite movie or favorite song. We'll never find the elusive one hundred percent. In any given competition there is something for every taste, preference, or opinion and everyone does not have to agree. Jeff Namian once described a finals competition as a play in several acts. Some people prefer act one; others act four, and someone might even enjoy act eight. It's a wonderful thing and the approval from the majority of attendees is exhilarating, but it's not always the case. And then there are those individuals who feel that it's their duty to let you know just how much they disapprove of your work. Be it a bully tactic or some form of self-validation, they often, by any means necessary, want to make their feelings known. I never, ever, mind someone having an opinion, but when it turns ugly or mean it's a different story.

With the 1986 Spirit of Atlanta Drum Corps show, the boys in the color guard removed their shirts for a scene involving people taking to metaphorical water in a celebratory baptism-like reference. Some people reacted to the sheer shock value while others saw the reference in context of our southern roots. Seeing the bare chest of young men is nothing unusual to drum corps rehearsals and certainly not unusual for the dance and theatre worlds. But bringing this kind of imagery into drum corps prompted a response from the editor of a well-known drum corps publication. I was twenty-six, still young and desperate to explore and figure it all out, when a letter arrived at the corps office shortly before the end of our competitive season. Not only a scathing review of my work, the letter, through contemptuous scorn, elevated this one-minute portion of the program to the downfall of the drum corps activity as a whole and my part in it unforgivable. *Really?* This portion of the show was not a fabricated or contrived moment merely inserted for shock value. Although I certainly don't mind a bit of shock when the time is right. But the choreography was certainly not lewd or sexual at all, it was actually pretty short and to the point.

My mind was racing and I remember thinking of the acerbic resistance when dancing became more prevalent in color guard. *Stanley Knaub and the Seattle Imperials*. The same venom was unleashed when color guards moved from military uniforms and boots to more theatrical costuming. *The Blue Devils introducing the famous sequined jumpsuits*. And the plan was never that shirtless would become any kind of trend at all.

    I immediately brought the letter to the attention of Freddy Martin, Director of The Sprit of Atlanta, as well as Tam and Sal. I sought out parents who served as support staff for the corps. I even called my father, a longtime deacon in the church of my youth. I received unwavering support even though I insisted on completely rethinking my position and taking the discussion far beyond what was required. And I often think that if that letter weren't so hurtful it might have been far more effective in altering everyone's opinion. But here in writing was a man stating his intention to "boo" the performance on his next viewing. (And no, that's not a reference to the well-known, very respectable drum corps writer Michael Boo). I went to the performers and was open to the fact that they might now feel uncomfortable and when we arrived at Championships in Madison, Wisconsin I asked the boys how they felt about performing this section of the show. They were resolute in their commitment and the show was performed as intended at finals.

    The incident reminds me of one of my favorite audiences of all time. Spirit performed on July 4th in Columbia, South Carolina for an audience completely made up of military servicemen and women. My concern for the response had nothing to do with guys going shirtless, but with the general idea of presenting drum corps, dancing and spinning flags, rifles and props. I had no idea how this particular group of people would respond. I was prepared for the worst and I cautioned the performers that the reception might be a challenging one. I anticipated the catcalls, the name-calling, and the dislike for the presentation. I stayed close to the field preparing to pick up the pieces of our morale. I have never been more thankful that I was completely wrong. These incredible servants of our country were nothing less than respectful in the celebration of what we performed. And then there was the interesting bonus: When the beautiful female performers would take the spotlight in the show the male audience members would erupt in approval. And…that moment of the male dancers baring their chests? Well, suddenly the female military servicewomen had their own moment of thunderous support. It was a genuine, honest reaction born from, I'm sure, these brave women inhabiting a male-dominated military. It will live in my memory forever. Never underestimate your audience.

Different regions of the country provide a variety of audiences also. So even beyond the makeup of the audience changing due to various individuals, different places around the country or world for that matter can redefine any given response. And as much as fans can have opinions about a given performance they can also have rather strong opinions about other audiences. They can quickly tell you why a particular part of the country responds this or that way and some audience members will explain why an audience half way around the world responded. If the old maxim announces that everyone is a critic, it only seems possible that even members of an audience can define one another. Regional bias is nothing new. East versus West versus Midwest is old news when it comes to drum corps and color guard competition. We see it all the time in major sports. Fans growing increasingly strident in their hatred for another team have even resorted to violence and nastiness in ways that dangerously redefine competitive sports.

The Bridgemen, long known for wanting their drum corps shows to play to the audience first and foremost, could put on genuinely entertaining programs and receive wonderful responses anywhere around the country. But I've also seen a segment of the audience reject them even to the point of name-calling.

The San Jose Raiders, from San Jose, California, were six-time WGI Champions known for their innovation. Like so many innovative groups, their contributions live on in performances we see today including the use of vinyl floor coverings. This floor covering could suddenly transform the gymnasium or arena floor into a theatrical stage. The staff there experienced a variety of reactions. The Raiders often took the road of originality and set a standard of modernism through choreography, soundtrack, concepts, and staging. Throughout the years the shows varied from *Romeo and Juliet* to Jack Kerouac poetry to Vivaldi. I joined the staff in 1990 and we would travel each year to the first regional competition in Boston, MA. Now, Boston audiences have a long history with indoor color guard and are knowledgeable and opinionated. We always knew going into this regional that we should be prepared for any kind of response. In 1992, we had decided to present excerpts from the movie soundtrack *Good Morning, Vietnam*. It was full of variety, breakneck speed changes, theatrical character, and humor—lots of humor! We prepared ourselves knowing that this knowledgeable audience might not prefer the irreverence of our presentation. We waited backstage to make our entrance into the preliminary competition. We kept it light, played around, and basically ignored the fact that we could be walking into the lion's den. The opposite happened. The audience laughed and was genuinely surprised at all the attributes we knew could exist within a fast-paced program of this nature. It was unique and it was fun. They let go of any regional bias they may have carried and honestly went along for the ride. It was a risk-taking moment bathed in excellence. The audience can often surprise you.

We've all heard the "boos" of an audience when the scores are announced. Now a lot of those people will say that their response is meant for the judges and not the performers. Unfortunately, those judges have usually left the stadium already and know nothing of the response unless they just automatically expect it. They don't stand there and take the noise like the performers do. And I've always felt that if you really want to show your displeasure with results, go and support your favorite group by making purchases from their souvenir booths, or volunteer, or make a donation. It's difficult enough to financially keep a drum corps or color guards afloat, and as much as they appreciate the verbal support, what they really need is to buy food, gas, or costumes and equipment. An audience's hatred for another group, or competitive results, or judges, does not pay the bills. The support of patrons, donors and volunteers can make dreams come true.

It still remains a fact that we are all members of the audience. Whether we are staff members, instructors, designers, judges, or performers, we are still a part of the audience when we are in the role of spectator. And each and every one of us wants to experience something in the process of observing. We want to feel something. We all have likes and dislikes, the desire to laugh or cry, to be amazed or surprised, to learn something new or wax nostalgic. Sometimes we want all these things together, jam-packed into one show. Sometimes we just want one idea to overwhelm and invoke our response. Some things suit us and others don't. And if there's anything that I wish we could all carry away from the competitive art scene, it's that just because we "like" one thing better, it does not mean we are required to "hate" the other things. And often I love performances that don't win awards, but that doesn't take away from those who do triumph from a scoring standpoint. I have had favorite performances that seemed like everyone's choice and at other times I feel like the only person who loves a particular show. It's all a wonderful example of the fact that just because something may not be your cup of tea does not mean that it's unworthy.

Again, ask everyone what is his or her favorite movie or favorite book or, worse yet, favorite television shows. See if any can agree on first place, second place, or third place. What was the top selling song of this past year? That would make it the most "popular" right? *Google that one.* Was the most watched television program this past year a reality show, a drama, or a comedy? What does that say about our culture or our choices? Are your preferences the same preferences of those people who make television their profession? Each of us, with our own point of reference, can find the common ground of appreciation. Everyone doesn't have to like exactly the same thing. It's an unfortunate ironic illustration that the very people who so diligently declare a love for what we do are the very people who often tear it down at a moment's notice. Defenders of what many may think are the "right" ways to create often are highly critical. Then, years later, they defend the very things they were previously so vociferously against. It's confusing for performers and designers to say the least. And competitive success can often breed an automatic rejection no matter how good the performance might be. But for every instance of rejection, we continue to strive for and recall those moments of sheer delight from an audience. And that may be what keeps anyone in the arts moving forward.

There's a lot about drum and bugle corps and marching bands that is simply loud. Now loud can be fun and exciting, but it is one volume level in the gradient of musical color. I remember hearing how incredibly bombastic The Marching Southerners could be when I was in high school. Boisterous volume, if handled correctly, is a thrilling experience, but so is soft and lyrical. But let's face it; whether it's the beginning, the middle or the end, we all appreciate a loud audience. Don't get me wrong; I appreciate a quiet, observant, emotional audience, too. But there is something wonderfully delectable about an audience that will show their gratitude with that level of commitment. And I have never heard a louder audience than the one at The World Music Contest in 2005. Drum corps is not limited to the United States. And Europe has its fair share of incredible groups. The World Music Contest brings together an astonishing variety of performances from all around the globe. We have seen marching bands, drum and fife corps, and even a bicycle band at this prestigious event. Yes, you've just read that right—there was a band playing musical instruments and simultaneously performing maneuvers on bicycles. It was amazing!

The Blue Devils have traveled internationally on several occasions so they were not completely unheard of within this arena. But here in the southeastern part of the Netherlands, in the town of Kerkrade, was the loudest audience I have ever heard in my life. It was exhilarating and one of those moments when I wish I could turn back the clock and jump into costume and perform. It wasn't just loud—it was loud on steroids. I can't even do it justice. That audience reminded me, and still does, of the possibility of appreciation, joy, and gratitude.

I hope I'm learning to depend less on what everyone thinks. The nature to please makes it difficult, but soon we learn that some people are just cruel. I have for certain learned to avoid looking at what anyone writes online in forums, or chat groups, or Facebook. It's an amalgamation of compliments to curses and innocence to evil. It's unfair for those people who are genuinely fans of what we all do and unfair to those people who are such important support for the performers. I've even taken to avoiding certain interviews after hearing moderators who had no interest in discovering answers, but only wanted to voice their own opinions. It plays like pandering to what they assume the majority of people are thinking as opposed to finding the truth and then letting people decide in their own way. New media options have produced an entirely new gauntlet. And fortunately there are still some writers out there who can still review a program with respect, intelligence, and thoroughness.

Ultimately I've learned the difference between the live audience and the online one. I'm hoping for the best. And even the live audiences in 2014 who booed the announcement of The Blue Devils in the night's competitive lineup, opened themselves to the actual performance and thrilled us all with a standing ovation. That says a lot for those people who may not be fans of a particular group or show, but are able to exhibit appreciation.

Audiences everywhere are full of individuals all with their own preferences, likes and dislikes, and particular taste. Just like creative people and just like the performers on stage. The possibility of magic exists in those moments where we find ourselves in the same place at the same time experiencing honest expressions of something we all love. Sometimes a show works and sometimes it does not, but we all seem to be aiming for the bulls-eye. It's all we can do.

CHAPTER 8

Compete

I've said it way too many times and I don't even pretend I was the first to say it:

"Winning isn't everything, but I didn't come here to lose."

I'm serious; I think I saw it years ago on a T-shirt or something. I wish I could take credit for the phrase and come across incredibly ivy league but alas, no. It is one of the most prophetic phrases I have ever heard and it rings of truth.

There is time enough for both winning and losing. The world will not end if we lose, our talent will not mysteriously vanish, and we will not be exiled to the far reaches of the universe. Life will continue and we will live to create again another day. If we are in a constant state of education, then losing is one more lesson that enables us to gain information that will hopefully help us to reach the inevitable. Now don't get me wrong, I'm not some sort of fan of losing. And I traverse the gamut of emotion and retrospect with as much heartache as anyone when it happens. Years of competing have certainly dulled the intensity of losing and given it a fresh perspective. There is something to simply knowing that this, too, shall pass and that hard work and the desire to "get it right" can, if we are completely honest in our process, provide answer after answer.

My deduction is that my childhood and growing up on the "outside" of society in general has compelled my need to overcome rejection. In other words, I'm aware of my need to compete for a way to fit in as well as my yearning for attention and approval in response to what could have been a debilitating existence. I like to win. There is also something to be said for the fact that I have always been privy to some wonderful friends and role models that enabled me to believe that there was something beyond misery. The smallest moments of affirmation can propel us forward in the largest of ways.

Competition gets a bad wrap. I'm not sure why because it seems like we are always competing for something no matter what the situation might be. And often we are competing for more than one thing at the same time. We desire higher scores, more attention, bigger audience attendance, public approval, and yes, money. And for all the times when competition is intrinsically essential, there are those who downplay its importance and relevance. Being competitive doesn't mean that a person cannot define competitive success in one's own unique way. Winning can be exclusively explained based upon one's own journey, a sense of longevity, and one's own expression of competition. Losing can do exactly the same. It can ultimately move one forward, backward, or result in a state of immobility. It's all information that will in some way spur a reaction. And how an individual reacts to winning or losing is ultimately what it is all about. Even though I do not always win, no matter how the circumstance might define it, I do not participate to lose. And there is no need to despise, disregard, or disrespect the winner because there is a chance the roles will be reversed before we know it.

The act of doing what we do is ultimately what we really desire. Our participation should, and can, remain the objective without downplaying or denying the competitive state of mind. A competitive state of mind does not require us to detest your our fellow competitors, create only by the score sheets, or disregard the abilities of the performers. It requires a condition of honesty that not only is open to creativity, but aware of our own limitations. It will always be to our benefit to know learn what we do not know. And don't enter a contest only to proclaim its unimportance. There is something to be gained from every experience.

The 1983 Skylarks winter guard production was a charmed one. One of those shows that was graced from the beginning with an ease and flow of creativity, talent and play—it was magic. I've been fortunate to work on several shows that evolved in this way: The Blue Devils winter guard in 1996; James Logan in 2001 with *Immortal Captive*; The Tate Chaparrals in 1989 with *The Science Of Modern Motion*; The Spirit of Atlanta Drum Corps in 1986; The Blue Devils Drum Corps in 1994 and 2003. These are a few examples where the process of creation was an organic, playful, flow of ideas and, though each involved an enormous amount of hard work, each show seemed to come to life with a sense of clear purpose. It by no means takes away from the joy of other shows and other years, but each experience is unique and sometimes it just comes naturally. I'm experiencing the same thing in this writing process. Some days the words come easy, full of flow and inspiration, while other days I pace the room reconstructing my hair.

We called the Skylarks show the "space show." Mickey's vision was, as always, detailed, complete, and there's a chance that he didn't experience the ease that the rest of us did while the show was nurtured and grown. Either way it was a fairy-tale process and the results were evident as the season unfolded. The Cavaliers winter guard was coming off a couple of incredible championship years and they were talented, friendly and admirable competitors. The season of 1983 looked as if it might be the one in which the all-female Skylarks would challenge the all-male Cavalier domination from Rosemont, Illinois. Jeff Namian and I were even able to contribute music that we had discovered while visiting designer Steven Covitz in Boston. I painted a parachute that became an interesting reveal of the performers in the beginning of the show. It was interesting, creative, imaginative, and proving to be successful with judges and audiences alike. That is, until the very last performance of the season in Dayton, Ohio.

That performance was like watching the figure skater that falls time and time again hitting the ice hard—in the slowest of slow motion. Not only did I feel the anxiety and desperation of the performers on the floor but, like any instructor or coach, stood helpless and unable to remedy the nightmare unfolding. I was dazed. *Were they overly confident? Were they too emotional? What had we missed in the training? Was this merely a lack of concentration? Was some unseen force of inevitability raging out there on the performance floor?* I couldn't figure it out. Their effort and technique were clear, but for some reason the glitches, fumbles, drops, and insecurity were governing this final performance. And as much as the instance is exaggerated in my memory, it wasn't the standard that they had set all season. I instantly knew there was a lesson to be learned, but had no idea what it might be. We were all devastated. They exited the floor and found refuge in a tiny locker room behind the arena. The tears flowed and someone tossed a roll of toilet paper into the center of the room. We watched it land on the floor and I still have no idea who provided that bit of symbolism to the events. We listened backstage as the Cavaliers brought the audience to a booming response. I made my way to a seat on the side of the arena floor with Tam on one side and Sal on the other. They consoled me all throughout the exhibition of Woonsocket High School. *God, drama much?* Even through my tears I felt a sense of determination to never feel this kind of emotion again. I "Scarlett O'Hara'ed" right there in the stands knowing that somehow I had to find more answers. I would never "go hungry" again. So however melodramatic I was in the moment, I knew there was something to be discovered and that losing was not the end. The next year would prove that the performers from the Skylarks felt the very same resolve, and they went on to win the 1984 Championship with the kind of spirit that showcased their determination, talent, and desire. I like to think that the 1984 Skylarks happened because of the 1983 Skylarks. They learned to focus in a way that I still encourage and teach to this day. It also helped me to define the difference among designing, instructing, and coaching.

Designing is a creative process and instructing disseminates pertinent information. Both are interactive for me and carry a deep sense of involvement. Coaching, however, really requires you to get into the heart and soul of the performer to help him or her realize a result. It's a bit like someone writing a speech, someone teaching you the mechanics of giving that speech, and then someone spending time helping you to understand and execute the speech. Let's say you buy a new bookcase. Someone designed that bookcase and someone then wrote the instructions for how to assemble the bookcase. And if you're lucky, there is someone who helps you understand the instructions and guide you through the assembly process. Does that make sense?

A few years later in 1986 I began a four-year stint at Tate High School in Gonzalez, Florida. It was a dream job with an outstanding marching band and color guard program under the direction of Bill Slayton. Tam had been an assistant director and produced the guard there in the early eighties so there was a feeling of legacy and I felt a strong attachment to the program. The band and guard, full of supportive and loving parents and boosters, gave me the family atmosphere and the security that I desperately needed. I was allowed to develop the color guard, be creative, and build on an already renowned competitive history. It also meant living in off-season beach rentals during the school year. I would spend hours on the pristine beach in Pensacola, free to think, plan, and dream far from the crowds of the summer season. My family could come for visits and it was one of the last opportunities I had to spend time with my mother before the painful process of Alzheimer's began to take its toll. It was a little slice of heaven and the members of the color guard were talented, beautiful, and full of personality. It was another one of the groups that I had long admired from the outside and these wonderful girls did not disappoint. I wanted as much recognition as possible for them, be it at school or in competition. I knew they deserved it and the quest for WGI's gold medal began.

I really enjoy working in the scholastic classes at WGI. I like the stability, the routine schedule, and the focus that a secondary education program can bring. There are challenges for sure, be it with athletic departments or administrative conflicts, but when you find yourself in a supportive system the results are amazing. My time at Tate was one of those instances. The support from administration was similar to the time I spent at Logan, with superintendents and principals providing an admirable lifeline to what other schools might consider a passing fancy.

On one occasion an angry, and probably jealous, basketball coach at Tate padlocked the gym doors during a holiday break when we were scheduled to rehearse. Before I could even fully express my disappointment, the principal, prompted by a parent's phone call, arrived at the school to quite literally cut the chain from the door. That sense of small-town support made for big dreams. Several principals from Logan have made the trip to WGI Championships to witness the achievements of the performers as well as the magnitude of the event. The promotional capabilities of marching bands, percussion ensembles, and color guards are valuable. They are a public relations goldmine. And I know the same can be said for any part of the music, theatre, or arts programs that travel in order to exhibit their talents and education.

OK, back to The Tate Chaparrals: I was on my own at Tate for the first two years with no additional staff and an expansive membership of seventy-five to eighty girls during the fall season. It was a huge program with a historical reputation. The Tate competitive winter guard is one of the oldest in the country founded by musicologist Michael Strasser and I was pretty green when it came to designing an entire show all alone. I was fortunate to have the help of the previous designer/instructor Roy Lancaster as well as Tam, Sal, and Sal's wife LuAnne. And so our competitive quest began knowing that we would be up against several other honored programs throughout the country. But one particular program that I admired, loved watching, and always took notice of was that of Union High School from Oklahoma. If we could even be considered in the same league with this incredibly effective program then we would be on the right track. Led by Alan Muggenbourg and Wes Cartright, the Union program was a prime example of how I can be a fan and a competitor at the same time. It not only makes competing enjoyable, but it also provides the opportunity for constant learning, and most of all, inspiration. I want two things from a champion, to build on the standards set by previous champions and to inspire us all to greatness. It keeps us all moving forward while respecting the past. The Union winter guard was amazing, to say the least, with challenging presentations, innovation, and unbelievable spectacle. By the time The Chaparrals finally achieved the gold medal in 1989, Union High School was not competing. But I like to think it would have been an amazing event with two astounding, highly respected artistic and athletic programs.

And now a story about tears…

1987 was a year for learning the art of restraint and subtlety. I designed a program for Tate based on the journal of a frontier woman during the early discovery of the western United States. After the season was complete I realized that in my youthful exuberance I had included far too much narration and basically "tried too hard" with the choreography and writing. I was artistically and theatrically immature. Hindsight is 20/20 for sure, but I like to think I would do it differently now and it certainly was a show that was tailor made for the young women at Tate. The show, *West of The Medicine Wheel*, gave the performers a chance not only to showcase strong equipment and movement vocabulary, but also to showcase character that evolved throughout the presentation. Remember that lesson from the 1983 Skylarks? I was determined to coach the performers to carry a "game face" onto the competition floor. I didn't want their emotion or excitement of the WGI event to overtake the job they had to do. It's something that I still believe today. Take each moment as it comes and do your job. Do not permit foreign thoughts to creep into your concentration while you are performing and be totally, steadfastly "in the moment." There would be no celebration or emotional exercise prior to entering the floor. We could be relaxed, but we would know exactly "where" we were and "what" we had to do. Do your job.

Prior to finals, with the last instructions and guidance complete, we made our way to the tunnel to await our entrance onto the floor. I usually walk to the front and take a look at the audience, get a feel for the energy in the room and keep tabs on timing. I turned around to take another look at the girls and see how they were doing and I panicked. They were in tears. It was an emotional nightmare and I had no idea why they were suddenly so unfocused. This could be a devastating obstacle as emotion can often overtake technical training and throw unexpected surprises into a performance. I quickly found a couple of veteran members and asked them why everyone was crying.

Their reply was priceless: "We're in character!"

I had to laugh. They had taken it upon themselves to totally commit to the opening narrative of the show. I had to trust them in that moment. Trust and love. Trust and love. But I'll never forget the tear ridden rhythmic reply…

"We-e'r-e in char-ac-ac-t-er!"

In this age of public scrutiny and anonymous posting on the Internet, a lot of people get accused of writing for the judges alone or solely designing for the sheets. It's a perplexing statement and usually made by someone who has neither the courage nor the experience of having created something that could deliver the performer's talents. That being said, I can honestly say that the judging philosophy is only one consideration in my personal process. It would be irresponsible of me to ignore the very thing that permeates the competitive arena.

Part of my ambition is to transcend the score sheets, which inevitably involves exploration that far exceeds what is presently there. Everything that we appreciate, musically or visually, at one time or another had to have its first exposure. Your favorite moments all had their first time. And where would we be had creative people or skilled performers not offered a brand new idea or skill for that very first time? There was a first time to hear the music of *West Side Story*. There was a first time a "company front" was exhibited. There was a first time that a flag suddenly could be spinning. Everything we hold dear had its initial moment and transcended the previous expectations. The act of questioning the norm is the motion forward, even if the result is successful or not. So it is one thing to know the scoring system and quite another to know it well enough to exceed its boundaries. More often than not I am certain that the great acts of innovation were accomplished out of an honest desire to communicate the unsaid. Being contrived and forced (which, yes, I have been accused of) is detrimental to the sincerity of a creative offering and is usually unable to be masked or mistaken. It happens, but it is an obstacle that I dare say we all want to overcome.

I love the research part of the process and I spend a lot of time finding inspiration in related subjects to the current project. I read related materials; I study the history or varied interpretations of the music. I look to the dance world, the art world, and the incredible resources of fashion. I look at related sports that may have tackled similar concepts. I save photos, tear pages from magazines, sketch, doodle, and look for any and every informational clue. I look to the past and the present. Research can spark something in the head or the heart. It also helps to begin to form an approach or feeling. But there comes a time when the research has hopefully found a home somewhere in my subconscious and I can forget about it and simply trust that I am standing upon its foundation when the real work begins. The research is there constantly to answer questions that arise or provide insight if a roadblock occurs. Research and information are not there to dictate, but to bring a genuine sense of substance. They are inherently alive no matter how simple or complex the subject matter might be. And there is certainly any number of ways that one can research. Some shows require more and some less. The creative process can involve releasing everything you know and starting with a completely blank canvas. So maybe the ultimate definition of the creative pre-production is simply preparation.

Nevertheless, we are, more often than not, in a competitive environment. With drum corps, my knowledge of the scoring system comes and goes, informs and vanishes, becomes obsolete or drives the possibility for achievement. I am aware of it, but not ruled by it. And to be honest, there have been years where scoring changes have occurred that I left unstudied until a point in the season revealed a judge's decision that I needed to understand. Often we are still developing the program while the competitive season has already started and lately I have taken to not listening to judges' commentary during that time. I don't want their limited knowledge of our specific process in my head. There's no way they can truly understand where we are on our path of uniquely individual development. Remember I am north of fifty with a few years under my belt, so it's not something I recommend for new designers and instructors, but it has helped me to focus on the performers, the audience, and the intent of the show. I will however listen to feedback from the staff and from judges during a critique conversation. Sometimes the dialogue can be quite revealing. And there are some wonderful judges with incredible experience that temper their analysis with context. They offer opinions I have learned to trust as much as anyone else. So I'm not sure what "writing for the judges" means beyond the fact that I am undoubtedly aware of "where" we are and "what" we are doing when it comes to competition. I know there are certain skills that I want the performers to showcase and I will always include those instances that provide them the opportunity to deliver the goods. However, being overtly driven by any scoring system inhibits the ability to transcend it and to offer what could be those cherished, innovative moments. What if Bresson never had a character look directly into the lens of the camera? What if Klint or Kandinsky had ignored the potential of an abstract vision? Ultimately, we have to choose our words wisely and master the tools of the medium in order to communicate whatever our message might be and yes, compete.

The winter guard process is a bit different for me. I've served, as many designers and instructors, on various committees that help to develop the scoring system and its philosophy. Lately, I've done some judging that also requires me to be much more aware of the scoring application. Designing requires, in my case, a global view. It requires having to look at the complete product and not single out one specific area or caption. But again, nothing dictates the design process more than the urge to present the performers through an interesting, creative, original, and yes, hopefully entertaining vehicle. I am conscious of the skills we need to present, mindful of how those skills can be embellished, but all the while sensitive to the fact that their packaging can create a moment that represents where we have been and where we are going.

Partly because I am also a fan of marching band, drum corps, and color guards, I will at some point throughout the competitive season watch competitors. Another result of gaining experience is knowing when and when not to watch the other performances. Different staff members handle those responsibilities well and it frees me up to concentrate on the creative and coordination process. I do like to hear what the other performances are about or what judges might be saying about our process. But there is a rule of those reports that has become imperative to me: I don't want to hear what is wrong with our competitors—I want to hear what is right about them. When I do begin to watch the other competitors I'm much more interested in what they are doing well rather than the unfinished or underachieved. Think about it: If you are running a foot race you don't want to know how slow the other athletes can run, you want to know how fast they can run. This certainly doesn't mean that you can't have an opinion, but if you want to compete you had better know what's worthy about your competitors. It's best to resolve yourself to the fact that a competitor does not have to be your enemy.

CHAPTER 9

Friend/Foe

Tam Easterwood could be a master of strategy and had an indelible confidence. He enjoyed competition and was mindful of the metaphorical race we inhabited. Even with a genuine deeply personal artistic vision, he was aware of what it meant to surpass his competitor. Tam worked hard at his craft. His confidence was perhaps a result of that work and the sheer desire to be the absolute best regardless of scores or opinions. I draw on that very confidence constantly whether I am at the start of a new project or speaking to the guard before a contest. I hear Tam's voice in my head pushing me and urging me to believe in myself. Having faith and courage is a big part of any game and Tam's certainty was a virulent whirlwind enveloping anyone in his path.

I believe Tam's contribution to equipment writing, technique, athleticism, and movement for musicians is undervalued. It lives on to this day and was a forerunner of our current state. It's clearly evident in State Street, The Spirit of Atlanta or the work he did at East Coweta High School in Georgia. And he did it all with sophistication, passion, and excellence—and never, ever at the expense of competitors.

Throughout our years of collaboration the one word that would best describe Tam and me is obsessed. During those years with The State Street Review or Spirit, we spent hours and hours discussing and dissecting the process. Over dinner or drinks, long car rides, or hanging out, it was discussion after discussion and quite often left anyone else around feeling totally ignored. We dreamed, we laughed; we planned, strategized and translated it into active, realized practice. I can't explain what made us able to work together so well. Friendship, I'm sure, played a big part. But our friendship had endured even throughout those times when we were competing with one another.

There was a time when Tam was with the Madison Scouts and I was with The Bridgemen. During a few WGI seasons Tam was with State Street when I was still with The Skylarks. Tam was also with State Street when I began with the San Jose Raiders. And there were summers as I began with The Blue Devils when Tam was working again at Spirit. The fact that we could be supportive of one another's work and genuinely happy for the resulting success was a given.

Jeff Namian and I had aged out the same year when we moved on to teaching drum corps. Jeff with the 27th Lancers of Boston and I in Bayonne, with The Bridgemen, I can clearly remember the tennis match of a conversation after both groups would perform on summer tour.

"I think you guys beat us tonight."

"No way, I think y'all were better tonight."

"No. You guys won tonight."

"No, you all did. I'm sure!"

You can guess which part of the conversation was mine. Bobby Hoffman was amused watching me walk over to the Lancer equipment truck with Jeff, picking up a flag and spinning it. He chuckled as Jeff followed me to the Bridgemen equipment truck and did the same. I remember Bobby telling me how cool he thought that exchange between two competitors was. We were friends, so I took it for granted.

Some nights the after-performance conversation went like this:

"I think y'all won tonight."

"Yes, I think we did."

Then there was this version:

"I think you guys did it tonight."

"Is there a bar around here?"

Preparation time or the "warm-up" before a competition is a show unto itself. No one pulls bigger crowds at this time than drummers. Running through their various paces, exercises, and segments of the show, they draw huge numbers of people filming on their cell phones or simply enjoying this show before the show. It's exciting and an opportunity to get up close to the performers and their staff. It's impressive to say the least. It's been nicknamed "the lot."

All the sections go through their own pre-performance process. Color guards, full of personality and the theatricality they are so well known for, have their own routine to get the bodies warm, ignite concentration, and engage larger-than-life communication. More often than not, facilities require most of the color guards to go through this process in the same area. Color guard, not unlike many sections, has a special brand of community. And even though we may be competitors on the field, this "warm up" time has often been a friendly, supportive time with everyone knowing that we all ultimately just want to have the best performance we can have. A tiny slice of life-like opportunity to share some common ground and gravitate to those competitors that, although quite technically and stylistically diverse, become friends as you travel from contest to contest. It's nice to see friendly faces at the warm-up. Whether they just wave hello or shift around to make room for you to start your own routine, most color guards have steered clear of pre-show mind games. Sure there are those that have strict rules about not speaking to another group or smiling at a friend. But I have found that competition is on the field and there's no reason to expend this energy or any kind of animosity during the warm-up. It's easy to stay focused, prepare oneself, and still be professional, friendly, and considerate. Fear and pressure during a warm-up can breed insecurity and a warm-up gone wrong can nearly guarantee intensity spiraled out of control. Different instructors and coaches have varying opinions of course. Tam used to swear by making the performers sweat as much as possible during the warm-up, the mindset being that they could work all excessive, nervous energy out of their system. Some groups run this time like a rehearsal, full of corrections and constant reminders. I've seen some groups have this time planned out like clockwork, even performing choreographed routines. I've also witnessed the ironclad brutal comments that some instructors/coaches make during this time inevitably stripping down the performer's confidence. I've seen short warm-ups and long warm-ups. I've seen relaxed and I've seen strict.

I remember Bishop Kearney High School's winter guard, one of the best scholastic champions WGI has seen, go into individual warm-up time and then come together in small groups to work short segments. Their instructors kept a watchful eye with minimal comments and strong encouragement. I really respected the results of their process that I saw on the competition floor. The year 1997 would be the first that I was with James Logan at WGI. The equipment warm-up area was small and the Logan rifle line ended up right next to the Kearney rifle line. It was a chilly concrete loading dock. They both ran segments as I cringed at the thought of the intimidation that could ensue. I had helped out at Bishop Kearney on a couple of occasions and loved their process, their performers, and their intensity. Logan was in a position to medal at this championship and I didn't know how they would react to these moments in the midst of such seasoned competitors. The instant was devoid of animosity and it actually energized the Logan boys in a way that I had not seen before. I think they realized they could hold their own and perhaps that they actually belonged in the upper tier of competition. The funny part is that this was a time full of trendy vocalizations when catching a toss. A bit like tennis players with their grunts and "ha" when striking the ball, it became a contest of who could perform the fiercest catch and the loudest "ha." They were confident, secure, and performing well so who was I to put the damper on the excitement. It was a moment full of respect and a testament to the statement that your adversary is not your enemy.

I start the warm-up with the body mainly because I follow a philosophy that nothing is possible without it. *Yes, Stanley Knaub.* As the years have come and gone, I lean toward a shorter warm-up and if we do have an extended period of time we relax. What the heck, I like to keep it relaxed anyway and music helps. Early season may include a run-through with the music during warm-up, but I'm adamant about the fact that marking parts is fine and the performers must be as physically economical as possible. I have abundant trust for performers who work hard at rehearsals so that preparation during this time is only about checks and balances, getting a sense of uniformity with the group and building confidence. As the season progresses, there's no longer a need for the run-through (during warm up) unless it's just a mental thing for the performers. Here would be another instance of Tam's wise and profound sensitivity. If the performers aren't confident you have nothing. He'd tell me often that even if things were going terribly wrong in those last few minutes of warm-up, he'd ignore it and praise them. It goes to say that in this vital stage of the process, animosity has no place. The surrounding energy needs to be friendly, positive, and inspiring.

Although I must say that when it comes to drum corps, traveling the country from show to show, venue to venue, that I hate looking for a place to warm up. I hate looking for space to warm up. You read that correctly. I repeated that point because that's how much I hate it! That's why I'm so grateful when I see friendly competitors. I cherish those times I have seen KC Perkins with The Phantom Regiment. KC's pre-show hugs are the best. I cherish my friend Marlieta Matthews-Beckman, with her smile and fun loving embrace; our history won't let us be enemies. I like seeing The Madison Scouts knowing that I have stood in the same place, or walking by The Cavaliers performing a dynamic all-rifle combination. It reminds me of home when I pause by The Spirit of Atlanta's guard and hear an instructor say "y'all." We really do all want the same thing, to reach our own unique potential. Good sportsmanship makes a complete competitor and one that others can celebrate because, be it night-to-night or year-to-year, everything can change.

Given the diverse personalities that make the roster of any team, there are bound to be some "bad eggs" in the mix. We've all had members with bad attitudes or examples of bad sportsmanship invade the development of a project. I try not to let those people be a reflection of the organization they represent because I've seen it happen first hand. Sometimes you are clear and succinct about behavior, rules, and professionalism—and sure enough there can be an individual or individuals that just refuse to comply.

And like any other job, sometimes you just have to let them go, release them, fire them, send them home, or whatever you want to call it. And after years of experience, I'm getting pretty good at recognizing a rogue personality versus the way they are being taught. And yes, I have seen the actions of instructors reflected in the members. The bottom line remains, and will always be, to keep your eye on the prize. However you define the "prize" from season to season, the key is to stay focused, respect your competitors, and make friends wherever you can.

Audience members with bad sportsmanship have changed the activity and so have instructors with bad sportsmanship. It's happened to every subjective sport throughout history. This is nothing new. There was a time when competing groups spent time together whether in social situations or pre-show preparation. I heard stories of the Scouts and The Cavaliers playing hockey. The Blue Devils and Santa Clara actually had a party cruise together for a couple of years. There was a time when friendly rivalries were just that. As a performer in The Madison Scouts, I remember warming up with competing corps. The two guards from two different corps circled up to share a warm up. It was a social experience and at the same time gave us an appreciation for our competitors. We went through various exercises with The Blue Devils and The Santa Clara Vanguard. I even found myself spinning one of the "bedpost" props from SCV. The female members of The Blue Devils were some of the friendliest we had met and I remember being amazed at how they all appeared tall and statuesque. Those friendships have lasted to this day and our off-the-field time with our fellow competitors such as The Phantom Regiment gave us perspective and the awareness that we had many goals in common. Along the way the times begin to change, and I think it became impossible to share this precious time. It's not out of the realm of possibilities that some staff members who became preoccupied with the "our way is better than your way" school of thought built an impenetrable wall that would not allow these experiences. When I began to teach, overhearing the vast amount of criticism from other instructors made me cautious and probably over protective. Instructors are not immune to the trappings of competitive bad sportsmanship any more than anyone else, so it became safer to drift to those folks that I knew would be respectful no matter the competitive situation.

Critiques occur at many shows after the contest has ended. It's a time for instructors and designers to interact with the judges and get feedback or offer further explanation. Often, it's a chance to make the case for more points. Rules and regulations have directed ethics and the variety of methods as to how this interaction can occur. But let's face it, we are all looking for ways not only to be better understood, but also to get more credit for it. It's still a contest. In the old days these were times of some high drama. From yelling to pounding the table, these could be some melodramatic situations that make someone with my nervous disposition run for cover. I'm not a fan of critiques because I'm usually still riding the emotion of the day we've completed, our results, and my preoccupation with the schedule for the next day. Critiques are normally very short and my predisposition is to use my "Scorpio wit" to come up with the perfect zinger to make my point. It usually backfired and still does as I find sincerity the best alternative. These days I'll walk out early before I go too far, but believe me, I'm sure some people can tell you some good stories at my expense. Now that's not to say that you cannot be totally honest about what you are feeling; in fact it's imperative that instructors and designers not hide behind a façade that can easily be perceived as pandering. That being said, I try, try, try to leave the drama elsewhere and hopefully getting older has helped me to funnel my emotions into a valid point. The judges' side of the table can be just as histrionic; I mean they are people, too, right? But the worst is hearing your fellow instructors or designers skewer your work like road-kill. I have overheard some seriously callous and cruel tirades that made my Scorpio stinger retract like the hair on a Crissy doll. I've learned to clear my throat or announce my presence. *Um, I'm standing right here!*

George Zingali, famed designer and larger-than-life personality, was infamous for telling us one minute how much he loved us then parading into the critique to proclaim our group's every weakness and fault. Somehow, I really think George actually believed both and though I would be shocked, I know we all miss his circus-like antics. He was genius, incredibly intuitive, relevant, and most of all, passionate. And his attacks, at least with me, were never personal. There is a difference. In fact, George Zingali, along with some adjudicators who have helped to shape the activity through their own work, was one of the first to tell me that I actually had a talent for what I do. Your adversary is not your enemy.

I've learned to be very careful because the person we may criticize after the show, whether live or online, could be someone we have to work with in the future. I have found myself in precarious situations where I've been hired to offer consultation or help to someone who has a history of dislike for my work. I'm not sure why anyone would declare their displeasure and then expect all to be forgotten when suddenly you find yourselves on the same side. Drum Corps are notorious for swapping staff from season to season. Staff members on opposing sides suddenly find themselves working with the same scholastic program. Performers come from philosophical divides to suddenly find themselves on the arena floor in the same production at WGI. It's one thing to have an opinion, it's quite another to be disrespectful. It's just a word of caution before I get too preachy.

The bottom line will always be that you want to compete against friends or at least be professional and cordial. There's no reason to go cannibal on your fellow instructors, designers, and performers. And, when all is said and done, it takes a friend to really tell you the truth when you need to hear it most. Your adversary is not your enemy. The enemy is that empty feeling at the end of any project that leaves you unsure of how to move ahead.

CHAPTER 10

Judge

We live amid a vast array of competitive pursuits. We've all seen the talent competitions on television from *Star Search* to *American Idol* or *The Voice*. I've seen championship competition for jump-roping and aerobics. Most people are familiar with figure skating or gymnastic competitions. Within figure skating there may be teams, pairs, or individuals. Within gymnastics, there's rhythmic gymnastics or even trampoline competition. There are dog shows, cat shows, and even bird shows. There's a variety in all these areas. There are contests for color guards, percussion, marching bands, baton twirling, and drum and bugle corps. Each and every one of these examples comes with some sort of adjudication—a person, or a panel of "experts," who can hopefully apply some sort of criteria to score the presentation. Judges come with the territory.

I think it takes a lot to sit in judgment of someone else's work. It's one of those mind-blowing thoughts that if I think about it long enough, I could never imagine doing it. Yet throughout the years I've judged marching band color guards, drum majors, drill and dance teams, winter color guard, and, many years ago, a beauty pageant. At first it was a compliment to be asked to adjudicate and I would participate through the nerves. These days I've learned to say no to those instances where I'm not ready, prepared, or qualified. I may be able to work with the criteria at hand, apply the system, and hopefully use the proper language, but I am still a bundle of paranoia second-guessing myself. Faking it is not an option. Now I do know that I have a wealth of experience, I've had incredible experts teach me throughout the years, I've listened to commentary for as long as I can remember, and still, judging is uncomfortable to me. I keep hoping that with more experience and more exposure I can become less anxious, but I know what it feels like not only to be performing, but I also understand the very personal, painstaking process that it takes to produce a work. These days I limit the assignments I take to those instances where I can muster the confidence and have faith in my own knowledge and experience. But as long as there are participants who desire to compete, there will be a need for qualified judges.

Being a choreographer or a designer requires a strong opinion, a point of view, and the ability to develop any concept that can exhibit a strong, definable editorial. It requires cultivating a unique approach that leaves your signature on every product and performance. It's a difficult thing to move from this mode of thinking into a judge's mindset that requires you to show no bias, be open to other thoughts, and then apply a fair, honest application of the criteria at hand. The best judges make this transition seamlessly and carry a deep, earnest, respect for what they are watching.

I have known some of the greatest adjudicators that our activities have ever known. It's impossible to name them all and I know there are judges in other areas of expertise that I am not familiar with. Two of my instructors, Sal Salas and Mickey Kelley, have worked as judges. I performed with Mike Turner and Jeff Namian and later saw their unwavering diligence when it came to judging. These seasoned, qualified, distinctly and individually driven people have built championship programs, taught championship performers, and made remarkable contributions to the art as a whole. They are not alone when it comes to the judging community. There are some true legends within the adjudication ranks. The ones I'd love to tell you about here continue to make contributions through their experience and expertise. Amid an era of an overly sensitive suspicious few, I won't put those individuals in the awkward position of being anchored to anything I write. I understand that I still work competitively and they are still actively judging; no amount of proof I could provide would enable the maliciousness to subside long enough to appreciate my compliments for them and see that these true adjudicators don't always place anyone I teach in first place. I will limit the name-dropping to people who have taught me at some point or that I have performed with or that are no longer adjudicating.

Shirlee Whitcomb has pretty much written the modern judges' book for Winter Guard International. Shirlee, throughout our multifarious history, has taken the cue from participants, competitors, and designers and put words to the thoughts and ideas that they longed to see as a valuable, honorable, and practical system of scoring. Shirlee was certainly not alone when it came to innovating the judging process, but she happens to be the person that I personally witnessed working diligently to further its development. We have certainly witnessed the influence of chief judges from Donald Angelica to Marie Czapinski and Mickey Kelly who have influenced philosophy and direction. Professional educators such as George Olivero have been able to offer a vast knowledge in a lasting and profound way. WGI's scoring system has taken years to develop and, although no system may truly be perfect, it's a thorough examination of what is occurring on the competition floor and is open to the future evolution that any system will require.

Great adjudicators are a diverse group of individuals, but there is a lot they all have in common. They have all experienced the competitive culture as teachers, designers, and judges. And most of them have competed at the highest level imaginable. Those that have cultured artistic strides in the activity have set aside their personal stylistic bias and kept the well-being of our future in mind. They have history, longevity, knowledge, and an incredible desire to see the pageantry world continue to grow and flourish. They all have strong personalities, have withstood the inevitable test of controversial decisions, and are part of the foundation that makes up who and what we all are. The greatest judges just want the scoring system to work and the performers to be ranked appropriately. And we have some real legends of the activity working as adjudicators.

OK, you can stop yelling at the page now. Perhaps you're thinking that I have somehow stood on the good side of all their judging calls throughout the years. Nothing is further from the truth. Refer to recaps throughout the years and you'll see what I mean. Marie Czapinski is one of the best adjudicators to ever work in the business. She was teaching with the Madison Scouts my very first year and even allowed me to write flag work for the very first time. My respect and adoration for her is endless and yet she can be incredibly honest about my work. She will not offer the accolades easily and expects you to work at the top of your game. I need that and I need her knowledge and history to keep me in check. And you don't get a ranking and rating from her unless she absolutely believes it.

It's important to remember that I have worked with champions many times *and I'm very proud of that*, but I've also worked with projects that were not in first place, *and I'm proud of that, too*. And the fact that I've been around long enough to consider many adjudicators as my friends does not stop them from…

A: being brutally honest if my work is not up to championship standards and

B: our friendship can often make them overly conscientious to counterbalance any accusation of politics.

It comes with the territory and what makes them strong individuals is their ability to work through the tough moments and hold fast to their own convictions. And there will always be someone on the downside of that.

And here's the advantage, if you choose to see it this way, to having a friend who is judging; they give you the harshest dose of reality. Sometimes it hurts worse to hear the honest critical opinion of a friend much more than from a stranger. It's easy to write off or disregard a stranger, but friends understand you and your passion in a way that counts for more than a passing comment.

Here's what I think most judges, friends or not, know about me; I will work to get it right. If I don't get it right this season then it will be the next. And if I don't get it right next season, then it will be the next. I've disagreed, I've whined, I've overreacted, but even though it may not seem like it, I do listen. Well, I listen to those judges who I think are in it for the right reasons.

The right reason has, and always will be, a genuine love for what we do. A <u>genuine</u> love for what we do. The right reason is always a sincere desire to see the results be fair and unbiased. The right reason will forever be an effort to further your own education and stay as current as possible in your area of specialization. The right reason is more "we" than "I." The right reason is the hope that we can progress, improve, and yes, move forward.

The wrong reason is to use the opportunity as an exercise in ego. Judges who want a power trip or some sort of validation of their own opinions are unable to clear their minds. Of course we all want validation and some sort of acknowledgement that our contribution, in whatever form, is worthwhile, but it's not a productive reason for decision-making. It's critical to have a clear head and an open heart and it's imperative to have a current, working knowledge of what you are judging. And that goes far beyond projecting your own unfulfilled competitive fantasies onto a reason to adjudicate.

Look, I played a brass instrument from the sixth grade until my freshman year in college. I play piano and have a decent ear. I've been around some of the best and brightest musicians and I can study the criteria like anyone else. I've composed music and worked with arrangers and orchestrators. There is absolutely no way I am qualified to judge music. To sit in judgment in this specialty would require me to have an ongoing, current, well-muscled, studied, knowledge of music. I don't have that. And I know I could not accomplish it by working a few days during the week and on the weekends. And it's not an area that I'm willing to dedicate the required amount of time and effort that would be beneficial to the performers, instructors, composers, arrangers, or audience. Is it any wonder why I am so concerned about judges working in areas outside their own practice? Judging requires a lot more than just the desire to be one.

I've heard it said that becoming a judge for some organizations requires "jumping through a lot of hoops." Well, yes it does. As designers and instructors, we spend every day working at what we do, not to mention the time when we're not working at it yet we're thinking about it. We are creating something from nothing, ambitious to find a truly original voice and translate those thoughts into quality training. Is it any wonder I would expect the same from the group of people who hold numerical outcomes in their hands?

The downside to being around for a while also means there are people who want you gone. OK, if that's too extreme, let's just say they want to exercise some kind of power over you. So for every time someone thinks that a "name" person gets preferential treatment, I can assure you there is a judge who wants to exert some sort of retaliation. From the subtle to the extreme, I've seen a lot of it. I've been told about conversations in the judging room where my name was tossed around like the bottom side of a garbage bag. I've listened to the insults cleverly disguised in commentary. I can work through it and pretty much get used to it, but ultimately the performers suffer at the expense of these judges. I've calmly sidelined myself while scoring systems were altered because of competitors or adjudicator's disagreement with our success. If you stay on your path, keep the faith, those judges (and yes, a few instructors) usually defeat themselves, get found out, or disappear for one reason or another. And most competitive sports have a process for submitting concerns and complaints. It's important for participants to be proactive when it comes not only to knowing the judging system, but also to voicing concerns over ethics or scoring application. The great thing about the WGI and DCI scoring systems is that they are guided and approved by competitors so there is something to be said for the fact that its evolution will follow that of the performers and designers. I've learned a lot from the good judges and I've learned what not to do from the bad ones. Really great judges have earned the opportunity to be…really great judges.

And now a story about understanding…

My second year with The Tate Chaparrals we attended the WGI Midwest Regional. At the time this was a premier event for Scholastic groups and it was fiercely competitive and a wonderful chance for early season exposure. Remember the show about Frontier Women that I over peppered with much too much narration? At this particular regional I had no voiceover in the soundtrack. I had wanted to present the narrative without any overt voiceover, working solely through the music of Aaron Copland and the choreography. I was ambitious in my hope that an implied story would satisfy the viewer.

I don't even recall our placement after prelims when it was time to enter critique with the judges. But I clearly remember this short critique with Jay Daly, one of the General Effect judges. The critique was held in a weight room at the school and I quickly mounted an exercise bike next to where Jay sat in a chair. I have no idea why.

I had respect for Jay, knowing that he had produced color guard in the past and he began the conversation with respect for me. He asked for an explanation of the narrative behind the presentation. I offered the story up and we began a conversation about what was clear and what wasn't apparent. The longer we talked back and forth, the faster I pedaled the exercise bike. Pretty soon I was in a full sweat and we were both laughing. But it's where the idea for narration came from and it actually did help judges, who sometimes only get one or two chances to view the program, to understand. It was one of those instances where there was mutual respect and I was open to problem solving. Now, if I could only have an exercise bike at every critique.

There are a couple of things that have driven me mad over the years. The first is when judges say, "don't take it so personally." I'm pretty passionate about what I do. *Duh! Of course we are going to take it personally.* I was glad to hear Isaac Mizrahi, acting as a judge on a reality television show, admit the importance of taking it personal. *How could we not?* Firstly, we are fiercely protective of the students and performers that we train. The Papa Bear/Mama Bear can come out if we think the performers are being undervalued or underestimated or worse still, insulted. Secondly, creating anything is deeply personal. And I am not talking about copying someone else's work; I am speaking of the genuine, uniquely divine, creative process.

For many of us, that process works on many layers from music, to staging, to choreography and costuming. So there are times when you cannot simply be held accountable for one aspect of the project, because multiple pieces of the puzzle have been born out of some mysterious place within you. It's indelibly personal.

In Las Vegas one year I had a young judge take a seat by me at a blackjack table. He was obviously amused telling me that the chief judge referred to our indoor competition as "just flags in a gym." Now whether or not this was true I have no idea, but it confused me. I've heard it said on many occasions and I understand the two-sided possibilities of its interpretation. I'm assuming it can be explained as a means by which we are not supposed to take it so seriously that we are no longer able to think clearly. On the other hand, I think it has been an easy way for someone to say that, when all is said and done, it's really no big deal. Well, if you haven't figured it out by now, it is a big deal to me.

Some of us have made this tiny cosmos of a culture our profession. It's what we do on a full-time basis. It's a career. For you, it may not be the most important thing in the world, but it's who we are and most importantly, what we are teaching. There's no need to be nonchalant when it comes to education at any level.

Now that's not to say that participation can't be considered a hobby. For many people it is a hobby, secondary to any number of higher-placed priorities. And the hobbyist can often be just as competitively successful and personally fulfilled as the full-timer. No matter what the time commitment or level of intensity, being realistic and honest is key. There will still be work to be done, and being aware of our own commitment can define our expectations. Being honest about our own limitations provides valuable insight. No matter what our level of participation, we deserve the very highest level of consideration.

The more I've worked as a judge the more I am able to equate it to performing. Even the best of intentions can't prevent a bad performance. Performers can drop equipment, gymnasts can lose a grip, figure skaters can fall, and I've had those judging experiences where I felt like I had done all those things…at the same time. It's a horrible feeling especially now that you know my arguably unreasonable standards for being a judge in the first place. Nevermind the numbers management, the commentary, or the recognition skills it requires—I continue to be uncomfortable with sitting in judgment of someone's work. *And that might be a good thing.*

So even if the best adjudicators are in it for all the right reasons, they are still human. I've heard of judges being sick to their stomach, battling nerves, or in tears with anticipation. And judges don't get a warm-up or a pep talk from the coach before they do their job. They are there to work and I appreciate those judges that, even after exhaustive preparation, can feel the same anxiety we do. Judges for WGI, DCI, marching bands, and most of the pageantry world do not work in anonymity. They are held accountable for decisions they make and if the system doesn't require accountability, I know many who exercise it personally.

So to those prepared, practiced, knowledgeable, respectful judges, I guess I would say the same thing I would say to any performer: You can be confident in your own history, your education, and your talent. That nervous feeling is not a bad thing. Use the nervous energy as a sign that you have respect for what you are about to see and know that you don't have to reach for that "astronaut pill" quite so soon. Breathe.

TEN (and)

As I have done some judging and provided overview commentary for WGI regionals, I have noticed a significant alteration to my observation of performances and scores. It's a very different experience when not sitting in the judge's seat. Evaluating the "what" and the "how" of a performance is transformed by where you are viewing and the fact that you are not bound by scoring criteria. Furthermore, the focus of a specific caption also requires crystalizing a very detailed mindset. Most scoring systems are designed in a way to let the totality of the system work while it addresses all aspects of the performance. Every performance has, to varying degrees, strengths and weaknesses. When working caption specific, it requires putting faith in that totality of the system hoping that, once all things are considered, the outcome will be balanced and fair.

Now add to those considerations that with most pageantry-related performances, judges are providing commentary during the performance. This causes an entirely different perspective and the brain works differently when one must consider verbiage as opposed to sitting in quiet observation. And, being human, judges are cautious of not offending, using the wrong tone, or speaking in perplexing language. It brings about an entirely new consideration while essentially trying to rank and rate.

So know that the next time you observe a competition or look at a recap of the scores that it's an entirely different experience when you sit in the judge's seat and are required to address the "what" and the "how" amid the complexity of today's programs.

Now that doesn't allow for differing opinions or everyone's right to prefer one show to another. It simply means that you can ask quite different questions about the outcome or a score when you understand the perspective of the judge.

However, I think it will forever be a question of what amount of experience, history, and knowledge allows someone to sit in judgment of any competitive program. If we hold our standards high in the creative process and we hold our standards high in the training of performers, it only seems natural that those involved in the act of ranking and rating would be qualified in a unique and honorable way.

CHAPTER 11

The Spinning Compass

By 1989 The Tate Chaparrals had finally won their gold medal. *The Science of Modern Motion* title was from an advertisement I had seen somewhere and thought it would be a wonderful springboard to explore all kinds of motion-driven scenarios. By this time, Skip Kelley had joined the staff and the performers were full of talent, technical prowess, and personality beyond the norm. They had the "X" factor. And if you've ever heard the term "hair-ography," I like to think it started here. It was the end of the '80s. My methods for their development didn't vary from what I had previously learned or what we were practicing at State Street and Spirit, nor did my standards allow us to accept anything less than the full realization of all our combined talents. Sal, LuAnne, Tam, and Roy Lancaster continued to be integral to the process and the show was a perfect match for the girls.

It was early days for me when it came to creating music and sequencing on keyboards. It was rough, primitive, and unrefined, but it served a purpose and I even sampled my own voice into the soundtrack. (Yes that's me speaking the opening statement.) I spent hours at the assistant band director's cottage apartment assembling the audio. Curtis Treadway probably noticed the worn-out carpet by the keyboard where I would pace endlessly trying to mimic the choreography I wanted to create.

I look back at that year now and I'm flooded with warmhearted memories and I love staying in touch with so many of those great performers. I probably overextended them and myself with the show, but considering the competition and following a champion such as Union High School, we simply had to go all out. We try our best to build on the past and move to the future. All things considered, the "what" and the "how" balanced in a worthy effort. *Hey, "all things considered" is a good title for a next chapter. OK. Write that down.* It's still the gold medal that stays with me everywhere I go.

By the end of the season something was pulling me away and off to something new. It's hard to explain that feeling of moving on. My mother had been diagnosed with Alzheimer's in 1985, I was quickly approaching thirty, and I think I could not come to terms with the fact that this might be my only option for work. It was difficult, but I moved to Atlanta and began to reconsider my future. It wouldn't be long before it became apparent that things were changing at the Spirit of Atlanta also. Changes in artistic direction, financial challenges, and staff indecision are not uncommon in creative endeavors and it was understandable that I would start to feel, along with my personal unease, uncomfortable with the situation. More and more, I was being put in an awkward position that involved decision-making that directly contradicted my position with the guard and my friends on staff. I wasn't prepared and I wasn't ready. It wouldn't take long for me to know that it was time to move on. Tam had already taken the summer off and was enjoying his free time until we got another request.

Our next step was spending a bit of time with The Cadets of Bergen County, formerly known as The Garfield Cadets. Once again I would be amid the creative, innovative minds that I had respected so much. The show was *Les Miz*, from the well-known musical, and it would be the beginning of a rich history of color guard awards for this Drum Corps International trendsetter. Watching how the process developed for them was another eye opener for me. Everything is a learning opportunity, right? I learned a lot. It was also another one of those groups who had larger-than-life personalities, on and off the field, staff as well as members. It was a great experience for me and just what I needed. I was a sponge watching Marc Sylvester work, I studied Denise Bonfiglio and Peggy Twiggs, and I was amazed at the creativity of Greg Lagola.

After the summer came to a conclusion, it would be decision time for me again. I was lucky to have quite a few offers. But some of those offers would involve moving away from Georgia. Mike Moxley flew me out to California to meet the folks at The Blue Devils. I was in talks with Jim Mason about the up-and-coming Star of Indiana. Spirit desperately wanted to rectify the situation. And George Hopkins, after offering me a much-needed retreat at The Cadets, wanted to make the position permanent. Pageantry people don't have agents, managers, or business types to guide us and this was going to be challenging and confusing for so many reasons. I tortured everyone I could with request for advice. And I spent the most time talking to my father. *How could I move away with mother being ill? What if I was needed at home?* This would be a guilt-ridden choice, not only for my own well-being, but also for those closest to me. My father's counsel was meticulous and thorough. For as little as he knew about drum and bugle corps, he loved the Blue Devils, but he also loved Spirit with their southern roots and the fact that I could be home. By the time we had "carouseled" ourselves into exhaustion he finally let me know that I would only be a plane ride away.

On plenty of occasions, looking back, I have been at the proverbial fork in the road. I don't exactly know how I feel about pre-destiny, but I sure know these instances have made a good argument for its existence. When I moved to New York City in 1982, I had been accepted into a theatre school. I made my way for the first day and peered around the corner of Broadway and 42nd Street in the direction of the school. This was long before the revitalization, for better or worse, of Times Square and the energy was captivating. This was the hustling, animated scene of some movie set with a rhythm of its own. I must have looked like a small child in a onesie peering around the corner of an oversized door. Something in me buckled. I don't know if it was fear or instinct, but I turned and never looked back to the school that could have offered an entirely different future. I am the first to admit it could have been stupidity, but then again, look what else I might have missed. In 1983, I was accepted for a six week intensive in Lake Placid, NY with the Twyla Tharp Dance Company. Twyla Tharp had long been an artistic hero of mine and this could be an unbelievable experience. This wasn't a fast track into the company, but it would be a chance to study with performers that I loved and Twyla herself. Unfortunately, it would mean giving up the summer with The Bridgemen and I was torn between obligation and opportunity. I did drum corps. The Star of Indiana went on to an incredibly fruitful competitive span of outstanding shows that included one of my favorites, 1993. They would eventually retire from DCI competition to become Brass Theater, and the award-winning production *Blast!* I continue to admire and be inspired by The Cadets. The Spirit of Atlanta has experienced resurgence. Wanting it all doesn't mean there's a way to actually have it all. It makes you hope that there really might be reincarnation. Maybe sometimes you stand at the fork in the road and both roads, both choices, are simply equal in possibility. Perhaps they are not good or bad, just different. And I think it's possible to have regrets and to not regret at the same time. Would-a, should-a, could-a: they're just more steps in the dance.

Thus, I packed my small car and charted the cross-country drive, with my father's blessing, to California. Full of anticipation and excitement, and a cleverly placed set of steak knives behind the driver's seat, I was heading west. *Would there be danger? Or sirloin?* Driving cross-country was enlightening and I understand the writer's yearning to put it into words. I would drive as much as I could during the day and find a place to settle down for the night. My favorite motel was close to the California border. The tiny motel diner was packed with holiday decorations while an older gentleman watched *Kojak* reruns on a small black-and-white television. I ate obviously reheated fried chicken to the sound of Telly Savalas's deep voice and a life-sized Santa Claus, surrounded by jack-o-lanterns peering at me from the corner. It was a storage room slash eating establishment slash Twilight Zone episode that made me smile. My room required you to turn sideways to enter due to the narrowness of its entryway. Every day and every night was absolutely different—and the trip, like the future, defined a new adventure. I arrived in California without incident and soon enough was off and running. My only regret of the trip was listening to the creepy soundtrack of *The Thin Blue Line* while I searched the desert for Interstate 5. I drove along the dark back roads of flatness while my fingers tickled the tops of the knives behind the seat. You can never underestimate the power of music, especially when it accompanies the voices from the documentary. *Thank you, Phillip Glass.*

My first year with the Blue Devils would be 1990. Like so many drum corps, color guards, and marching bands, I had been a longtime fan. I had been on the outside looking in on a perennial champion of the activity. I had also witnessed the kickback that comes with consistently being at the top of a highly competitive sport. There was even a time when there was a barrage, a full-on marketing ploy, of "anyone but the Blue Devils." I remember being aware of the rude, unsportsmanlike, ridicule that permeated the competitive scene. But I also observed the Blue Devils' ability to traverse the hostile terrain with grace and yes, with one foot in front of the other. It's happened to several groups throughout the years, not to mention artists, composers, athletes, writers, and pretty much anyone who does anything well. Here's the thing: Popularity can be fickle, so it's best to make it about the work. And work for me meant The Blue Devils, an incredible staff, star performers, and a chance to explore a new style and a new coast.

I knew going into The Blue Devils that I was going to be around some of the best minds in all the related activities. Since 1990, my role at the Blue Devils has evolved and responsibilities have multiplied and I would soon learn not only to trust the expertise and proficiency of the staff, but also Jay Murphy in particular. Jay, with a lifelong history in drum and bugle corps, is not only one of the most intelligent people I have ever known, but brings a strict palate of standards that is an invaluable resource. Jay has blended the ideas of concept, geometrical drill, and choreographed staging in ways that have virtually redefined the art. He also was one of the first proponents of the concept of motion as "process through time." One can watch a process from 2012 to see a traveling block give birth to multiple lines and events only to migrate into a parade on the opposite side of the field. Here is an example of each piece of the puzzle continuing to live on its own and morph gently into a new progression over an expansive and informative amount of time: A unison block formation with an outside frame that continues to decrease in size as the texture on the inside emerges into multiple thoughts and ideas as it escapes the confines of the square perimeter. A series of vignettes each with its own accomplished sense of shape and time. The simplicity of a powerful moment of bombastic brass marching backwards while holding a mass textured amoeba like form until snake-like tentacles begin to slither mysteriously outward like Medusa's head of snakes. All of this occurs with impeccable musicality and conceptual consistency, not to mention the advantageous placement of the musical voices. And all these moments are connected through time with just as much attention to detail as the event itself.

Throughout the years, Jay has pioneered methods that transcend the paper (where drill writers place ideas) in favor of a more three-dimensional choreographic development. Even beyond the incredible possibilities that technology has offered, Jay still requires the living, breathing action that enables the design process to make the most of the performers' interpretation. No longer are forms limited to mere set-to-set progressions as they seamlessly morph through time and often involve esoteric machine-like qualities that work on multiple levels. We live in a culture of marching band, color guard, and drum corps with a wide range of styles from the wonderful tradition of the Ohio State University Band to the outstanding precision of a Texas A & M Marching Band to the fantastic geometry and often thematically driven progressions of Michael Gaines to Jay's watercolored merging of ever evolving abstract visual thought. I appreciate <u>all</u> styles and methods, but I have witnessed Jay's contribution first hand. Jay, like so many of our illustrious staging and drill minds, came from color guard, so he has a certain understanding of bringing the spotlight to the "what" as well as the execution of the "how." And how one journeys through the duration of a performance, in its tiny moments as well as the totality, is a Jay Murphy achievement.

Tam often told me that the two rifle lines that influenced him the most were The Skyriders Drum and Bugle Corps (Lee Carlson) and The St. Joseph's Grenadiers winter guard. Jay was a driving force behind St. Joe's and when he was brought into The Blue Devils to take charge of the rifle line, Tam was an instant fan. Jay's position at The Blue Devils also evolved and he would continue outstanding work with winter guard competitors such as the iconic St. Anthony's Imperials and the emergence of the award-winning San Jose Raiders.

Here's a fun fact. We had met years earlier in 1986 when Sal had brought Jay as well as Stanley Knaub in to collaborate on The State Street Review production of *The Seasons*. In the summer of 1987, exhausted and a little worn out from touring, I was hiding out on a bus as the scores were announced at DCI finals. Jay was the person who boarded the bus to congratulate me on The Spirit of Atlanta winning its second color guard title. It was a classy move and he also made me not feel quite so guilty for having missed the announcement.

Jay was the reason I got to be a part of The San Jose Raiders and we would later work on a world-class winter guard for The Blue Devils. Finding new ways of thinking about process and presentation took precedence during these years and it translated to our additional collaborations. Again, the act of moving forward would provide the impetus and the search for a fresh perspective that could turn what would just be a job or a hobby into a shared exploration of transcendence.

Music educators and, in particular, band directors work harder than anyone I have ever seen. I've been privileged to work for and with some of the best in the world. From Dr. Walters at Jacksonville State University to Bill Slayton and Joe Hooten at Tate High School, their dedicated work ethic is a continual influence. Gary Gilroy, director of bands at Fresno State University, virtually drafted me to come and work at Beyer High School in Modesto, CA. His enthusiasm and energy was contagious. Ramiro Barrera moved to James Logan High School in my second year there. He has also worked as program coordinator and music coordinator with The Blue Devils. Ramiro, a larger-than-life personality, is a veritable musical authority. His artistic taste has served as a resource that still resonates when I am faced with choices and tough decisions. He has high standards and expectations that bring out the best in a person. And one thing I know for sure, these extraordinary educators protected and shielded me on more than one occasion from distractions that would inhibit and deter me from doing the absolute best I could. Conflicts of schedules, facilities, or the agenda of parents' concerns were often intercepted long before they became an obstacle for me. This was due to the strong leadership these music educators provided and the cooperation of boosters who held the concern of the students as priority.

So California was a good fit for me and began to feel like home. The map that brought me to this point was one of whims, gut instincts, and undeniable attachments. I had lived in Georgia, Alabama, Wisconsin, New York, and Florida while all along the way experiencing the vast array of regions our country offers. Through it all, and including the time since, I continue to understand my inability to take on more than I can handle.

Remember, I was that kid who could not garner a satisfactory mark in self-control. My mind churned, rolled, and existed in a state of whirlwinds from an early age. It still makes me yearn for a complete night of sleep. I came around long before there were diagnoses, studies, or techniques that could help someone harness that superfluous energy and constant barrage of ideas. By the time I arrived in California it was clear that I would not be one of those multitasking masters taking on too many projects all at once. I also understood, rather quickly, that even though it could mean more money I would have to define those times that required the greater percentage of my focus and those times where collaboration would be key.

I've never understood how designers could take the primary lead in multiple groups at once. When I dive into a project as the primary creative person then it requires every ounce of brainpower and physicality that I can muster. Even though I might be working on more than one project at a time, I am not in a lead role in each one. I also know those instances where I am choreographing the entire show and those instances where staging, production, music, and costumes become my total responsibility also. It's one of the reasons I've taken the lead only on three scholastic programs—Tate High School, Beyer High School, and James Logan High School. I couldn't even handle the "feeder" groups associated with these great programs. It took every bit of my energy to take on the world class requirements of their top groups. Add to this those projects where I was part of larger team and it's understandable that my time was full. Attempting to win multiple championships at once is no easy feat, not to mention the toll it takes on one's nerves. I was fortunate to have capable and dedicated help and know my own limitations in every instance.

I also would occasionally venture out to help friends with other projects. Not only could it be relaxing opportunity to contribute to another program, but I also knew that through the exposure to other methods and techniques I would continue to learn. I worked with Phantom in 1983 on *An American in Paris* at the same time I was with the Skylarks. I also began my tenure at State Street while I was with the Skylarks. I had for many years contributed to Blessed Sacrament because of my friendship with Jeff Namian and in 1990 they would be co-champions with the San Jose Raiders. I was honored and I was continually learning. It was never about who was better than whom because they were just different shows with different techniques and approach.

One of my most influential excursions was my time at Bishop Kearney High School. Vincent Monacelli, an icon of winter guard, brought me in to offer up some additional equipment ideas to an already stellar process under Sam Cappadonia. Vinnie's design process was innovative, fresh, and unique. The girls who performed with Kearney were some of the best I had ever seen. It was a holistic performance approach that possessed a sense of totality that I continue to hold as a standard. Even conceptually, the audacity required the same commitment and depth and the ideas would be fleshed out to the "Nth degree." And Vinnie would start early. Championships would barely be over before they were on to the next season's preparation. The summer was full of training, choreography, and concept development. I was never surprised when they would achieve high scores in the early winter months of the competitive season.

Not all staging is meant for the choreography that accompanies it and not every bit of choreography is meant for every form. Even though many of us knew this reasoning, and perhaps felt it intrinsically, it was written in bold capitol letters when I experienced Kearney's process. Knowing how different pieces can take the lead during the design process opens up the potential to an authentically communicated and fully realized idea. Understanding how the marriage between choreography and staging was imperative became a significant lesson for me, especially when I'm creating and designing the entire program. It also began to take on a deeper meaning through the simultaneous choreography of the body and equipment work. Harmony is not just a wonderful musical term. And when the technical proficiency of the body and equipment are equal one can discover the truest possibilities for communication. I have the highest appreciation for Bishop Kearney, not only as a competitor, but also because of what they contributed.

The Spinning Compass

CHAPTER 12

Inevitable

Collaboration is inevitable. One may feel, at times, dreadfully alone in the process no matter what the circumstances might be. But the truth of the matter is that we are not alone when it comes to any area that might fall inside the scope of pageantry. It's the magic and the great comfort of any of the aforementioned areas. Whether you are a performer or a technician or a designer, there are others who surround you and will, in some way, shape, or form, garner your consideration. Once you learn to embrace your part of the puzzle, your decisions will be influenced for the better, and your nerves, difficult as they may be, should find some consolation. *Easier said than done, I know.* Collaboration comes in many forms. First and foremost, it requires work with the performers/competitors. It may require work with a creative team or a technical team or both. It may mean considering the ideas of musicians, marching specialists, costume designers, or sponsors. There is a director or a boss. There is a support staff of volunteers who have given their time and goodwill to make sure the creative efforts or the wellbeing of the performers is in place. And there is certainly a relationship with the audience and the judges. These days, social media and marketing have offered a whole new realm of people to encounter. Cameras surround us and media savvy observers record so many of the aspects of what we do.

Working in winter color guard with The State Street Review was the easiest and most comfortable in my experience. A multifarious assortment of personality and knowledge, this collaboration was smooth, playful, and deeply heartfelt. We were all connected obviously through Sal and I think this gave the family atmosphere to the process. As the creator of State Street, Sal made it easy for all of us, performers and staff alike, to follow his lead, his creative direction, and his personality. For Sal and Luanne, the financial burden must have been incredible. But they held our trust, treated each of us with love and nurturing, and in return we were willing to take on any journey before us. Their creative and directorial evolution included all of us at various levels of involvement.

The State Street collaboration worked like this: Sal with a concept and setting the staging process, Tam handling the rifle choreography, and me taking on the rest. Luanne helped Sal with staging and expertly took on the artistic design of props and costumes. For many of those years, the shows featured original music by composer Rich Goidel. Sal's touch would be imprinted on every area of the shows. Neither Tam nor I lived in Madison, so writing took place on holidays and quick trips, some years more frequent than others. And Luanne, with her artistic eye and steady discipline, made all the parts work. The wonderful thing about the staff at State Street throughout the years was their ability to edit, embellish, or clean the work thrown at the talented performers. Tam and I felt comfortable leaving our egos behind. The product would always be in safe hands no matter who was contributing. With the exception of *The Seasons*, 1986, we pretty much had the process down pat even as new instructors would be introduced onto the staff roster. Again, the act of collaboration would produce a fresh take on the concept, provide a learning opportunity, and give the performers exposure to different schools of thought. Amazingly, it was another great example of ego being set aside in favor of creativity and trust.

My part of the State Street Review, beyond performing in 1981, would work in this manner from 1984 to 1989. Because I was charged with a hefty amount of writing and choreography, I was more than willing to put my faith in the staff to fulfill it. This was especially true about Luanne. I could often feel overwhelmed. Tam, however, took ownership in those rifle lines as only he could. It's part of what made him special. But there was a time in 1989 when he was learning to place his trust, however selectively, and collaborate in a new way for him. Tam trusted Tim Glenn, a former member and incredible talent, to realize moments where his imagination was outdistancing his own physical ability. Tim has since become an incredible artist/choreographer and continues to work at the university level and beyond. Watching Tam give over any degree of power to anyone was a great example of not only Tam's knowledge, but also Tim's ability to earn Tam's respect.

The comfort of State Street extended to the ongoing supportive atmosphere Sal and Luanne created to birth the work. *Eww, that sounds weird.* I know, but it's true that creating anything is full of self-doubt, insecurity, and basic paranoia. My preemptive routine has always included taking a moment to simply be alone and clear my head; I perform an intellectual tango in an attempt to convince myself that I am fully capable. Even now, after years and years of routine, it's still necessary. At State Street, I always appreciated the excitement and unconditional support that permeated the atmosphere. Nothing is worse than teaching something followed by no reaction whatsoever. I'm not saying I need full-on vocalization, but those moments where the air is heavy with absolutely nothingness are painful. Blank stares are like daggers and wandering eyes are even worse. Those performers and observant staff members are your first audience. In that moment it's easy to be deflated or energized. The State Street performers and staff could pull the best out of us with their optimistic, wide-eyed attitudes. Collaboration is a two-way street. And I was lucky when people like Carol Abohatab would bring her considerable talents with us to The Spirit of Atlanta for the summer season. Another one of those trusted cohorts, Carol was able to improve the product while supporting its purpose.

Process is a sensitive issue and after working with, watching, and learning from wonderful artists, I have seen how vision and collaboration take on many faces. Even in our culture of marching history, we can always look to the dance and theatre world at how some of the greatest have maneuvered the tricky artistic climb. There are certainly ups and downs, but understanding the collaborative aspects can enhance, inform, and fulfill the experience. There is a "give and take" that acts as metaphor to any relationship if not life itself. And different programs have called for different degrees of collaboration. Different pursuits of creating or rehearsing call for enabling the enthusiasm of others to take the lead while you recharge or take a brief moment to catch your breath. All of this brings to the forefront the amount of trust you must have in not only the process or the product, but also in the people around you.

Whether it was a result of functionality or simply an issue of time, I have, in most instances, taken on the choreographic responsibilities. Often it's a style consideration and a more efficient way to facilitate coordination of the elements. Those seasons of collaboration have not only lessened the burden, but have also given me a chance to behold the heavy lifting done by others. Working with other writers and choreographers has prepared me. Stanley, Ron, Tam, and the many choreographers at places I've worked on a limited basis are influential, skillful training for those times I have been charged with full responsibility. And to a larger extent, learning to have faith in those I've worked with ultimately can provide the faith, sometimes blind, in myself. I've quickly learned to ignore the negative voices with their doubtful interrogation, and proceed with the knowledge that I've found the answers before. I still hear the voices of those I have previously worked with whispering and encouraging me.

By 2003, my position at The Blue Devils Drum Corps would take another step. Because of my schedule and availability, and I hope my ideas, I would be asked to take on the role of program coordinator. The title, for me, is exactly how it sounds. Coordinating the creative efforts of the design team and providing direction as needed. I had previously interacted, on a creative level, with other sections of the corps. I had suggested show concepts like Club Blue in 1996 or sang musical ideas to Wayne Downey for "When A Man Loves A Woman." There were all kinds of contributions from staff members throughout the years, but I was beginning to learn a bit about all the areas in a holistic manner. It was not a conscious effort on my part, but one that didn't go unnoticed. Now, I would be in a position to elevate my understanding of collaboration to a new level. Daunting, as it seemed, I talked it over with several staff members, garnered some courage, and proceeded with caution, and yes, a lot of faith.

I equate the job in many ways to that of a magazine editor. It requires establishing direction and taking note of people's talents. The inspiration and ideas can come from a multitude of sources, not just one's own. It's important to let people do their jobs. The job doesn't require doing everything, but it certainly requires contributing, infusing, encouraging, and putting it all in perspective. I provide context. I reside at the steering wheel of imagination and inspiration, deciding how fast to proceed, or shifting gears, or charting course. I also know when to let someone take the wheel for a moment so I can rub circles on my weary eyes. I know when to ask for solutions, but I also have to be decisive when questions arise. Amid a bevy of self-doubt, I often fake the confidence and make mistakes just like anyone else. But it's my charge to keep the overall plan in mind and keep my eyes on the road ahead. When the surge of ideas comes rushing in, I depend on the concept to answer questions and delicately try to deliver rejection or unwelcome decisions. It's not easy. Psychology becomes as much a part of the daily grind as skill. The job doesn't mean having to do everything, but it does mean having to be aware of the totality. And it requires being aware of the, hopefully forward, momentum. At least that's the way I see it and I've certainly witnessed varying degrees of control and dictatorship while working on other projects. Some people don't want to relinquish any miniscule portion of the process. That doesn't work for me. Making the best use of each individual's talents and enthusiasm keeps the energy flowing. This is where I reside now and who knows how this will grow and change in the coming years. But there are reasons and instances that have taught me this approach and I think it's a welcome ideology when it comes to collaborators. I try to be decisive and definitive only as a result from the information I have gained from those around me.

And now a story about being unsure…

The idea for a show based on the journey of blues music and its relationship to railroads was one I had originally had in mind for The Spirit of Atlanta Drum Corps. The southern roots of that particular drum corps and the percussive nature of railway rhythms seemed a perfect match for Spirit, but one that never came to the table in their decision-making process. The timing was never quite right. That could have been a result of my position there or the personnel involved. In 2004, I brought the idea to the Blue Devils and there was enthusiasm and optimism for the essence of this approach. It had style and drive and the imagery was concise and imaginative. I am well aware of the ability of each part of the Blue Devils' team to examine and exhibit the concept through specific efforts. The concept not only resides in the brass parts or the percussion parts, it goes beyond the choreography or equipment writing and reveals itself even in form, drill, and staging. Taking ideas or basic "drum corps" tools that may appear from year to year and putting them into a new context makes, I think, the design highly original and specific to that concept. There are a limited amount of musical notes, but look at the vast, unbelievable combinations that have offered an infinite amount of universal communication. Look at how much music has been created and it's staggering to think that it's all based on a finite amount of basic tones. I love that. It's no different visually in drum corps and understanding the context of a moment can breathe new life into what could have been simply a repetitive moment. What can make a rotating block different in *West Side Story* than *Spartacus*? Context. That's given the fact that thinking a rotating block even belongs within the concept in the first place. Everything presented, from dance to color to drill, has character. It's something I believe strongly.

OK, back to the story. Historically, drum corps have loved offering the "new ending" for a finals performance. Sometimes to great acclaim and other times the execution falls flat. Adding something new at the very end of a season has always scared me. When the idea of The *Summertrain Blues Mix* first came about, I had always mentioned the train leaving the stadium, but the idea had never found its way into the design of the program. I had often discussed it as the battery, or drum line, departing the station because they were so indicative of the railroad sound. Somehow as we approached the final days of the season, the discussion shifted to the brass and the battery exiting the stadium. I was unsure, insecure, and indecisive on the entire idea. *What if it came across corny? What if it fell apart? What if no one cared?* I could not make up my mind as I listened to the multitude of opinions from the staff. At the beginning of one of our last rehearsals during championship week I commiserated with Jay outside the stadium. I posted myself on the parking lot curb, holding my head in my hands and rattled, once again, the pros and cons of the idea. Then Jay informed me that Todd Ryan was teaching the idea to the corps and we could look at it and make a decision. I think they all knew I was struggling and the only way to find an answer would be to try it. It's a hallmark of The Blue Devils in my opinion. That willingness to give the idea a chance and if it was right so be it and if it wasn't, we could forget about it and move forward.

Somehow I got a burst of optimistic energy. OK, let me take care of the color guard and then we can look at it. We got to work and the response was positive and the energy from the performers was excited and eager. It was enough to convince me.

On the night of finals we performed the new ending. It may have been one of the best endings ever at finals for several reasons. It was the appropriate ending for the concept and the performers were energized with the knowledge that they were offering a clever surprise. Metaphorical sparks illuminated the field like the railroad itself. And it was one of the most unique, and entirely new, audience reactions I have ever heard. Once the departure of the corps began to register with members of the audience, the audible reactions swept through the stadium in true Doppler fashion. The audible response literally "traveled" throughout the stands and resulted in a brand new kind of reaction. It was a surprising and impressive moment. It was absolutely thematic and appropriate, and superbly executed. My worry had been for naught.

Finally, I would learn that not only would I have to truly know the performers and the staff, but I would also have to recognize my own insecurities and know when to release my fear. We lost that contest (interestingly enough perhaps because of the scoring caption known as general effect) but gained a lot more than we could have ever imagined.

When writing, designing, or choreographing for marching bands, drum corps, or color guards or twirlers, there will never be a more important collaboration than with the performers or athletes. The more expansive their ability, the broader one's vocabulary can become. The more extensive their theatrical reach, the further one's emotional range can aspire. Simply stated, in competitive circumstances, the collaborator is there to facilitate their talent and their skills. Every step of the way requires taking cue from them. Creative aspirations and ideas must meet the performers somewhere along the way and merge into a unified sense of presentation. All the while, the job requires continuing the educational process that all these wonderful young people have joined to experience. The goal is to raise the bar as high as possible. It's definitely not all about you and your vision or your grandiose ideas. It's a partnership that hopefully is rewarding for everyone involved. And similar to an actor, the amount of oneself that reveals itself in a project can vary to different degrees.

The 1989 *Salsa* show with The State Street Review comes to mind when I think of performers taking the lead. The creative process, at least for Tam and I, was absolutely inspired by the talents of the performers that particular year. 1989 felt like a culmination of the preceding years with many of the same people involved. They were physical, outgoing, highly intelligent performers coming to the world of indoor color guard amid a whirlwind of pop culture fireworks. The references to music video, pop, and jazz dance as well as a new breed of movie musicals were as much a part of their daily lives as their technical and expressive training. It was inevitable, thanks to Sal, that a competitive program could be designed to showcase their unbelievable use of body and equipment as well as a strong masculine and feminine energy. Full of rhythmic nuance, character, and athleticism, watching them perform could turn into a rock concert atmosphere like it did in Pensacola, Florida at the WGI regional contest. There are still body/equipment moments in that program that are unchallenged today. Similar to my experience with Spirit in '86, here was a guard that was stepping into highly professional territory and it would have been a disservice to their talents had we not capitalized on it. We could not put them in restraints or attempt to tame the raw, outrageous energy. It simply became our job to cultivate it, frame it, and serve it up with challenge, charisma, and verve.

With the Blue Devils World Guard in 1996, the idea was to musically take a left turn from the previous year. How could we melodically offer something well known and relatable and at the same time test the boundaries of audio design? As the performers came together we began to rehearse the classic "Summertime" from *Porgy and Bess*. It was evident from the start, that here was a particular group of performers that was well versed in multiple styles and techniques. Stanley brought to them a level of dance training that evolved into a refined, and yes, professional approach. Behind the scenes, Stanley was taking notice of the capable performers and pushed me to mix my own movement take, more jazz-like, into the recipe. Suddenly, here was a group of performers serving notice to us as a design team that they were ready for a challenge. We would have to up our game. Jay, again with a stroke of genius, came up with a light bulb moment as we sat over drinks one night after rehearsal. We had been focusing on a singular interpretation of the song, which is fine in and of itself, but left Jay somewhat empty. He finally had the thought to bring three different versions of the same tune together. Finding a diverse trio of the same music would suddenly offer different stylistic, technical views of the same melody. The search began for the right arrangements and we were soon in the studio mixing and yes, mashing, the music into a cohesive piece. During the incubation period I would get to use a lesson I had picked up from Vinnie Monacelli at Bishop Kearney—go ahead and create choreography and combinations that could somehow, like puzzle pieces, find their way into the program. There were times when these combinations would take the lead for Jay to stage, and other times staging concepts would be "front and center." Both opportunities began to fit together into a well-paced presentation from top to bottom. All because we were astute enough to realize that these talented and extroverted performers were prepared to take us someplace we had never been before.

The same can be said for the degree one part of the design team can take in the lead through a project. Moments shift from music to visual to choreography. It changes often and adds fresh perspective. The impetus inspires and brings a focus and often keeps the spirit of innovation alive. Throughout the collaborative process, no matter the extent, every season can offer a broad range of method, approach, and concepts. It's the reason I also like to think one season to the next can be extremely different. Look at the San Jose Raiders winter guards moving from *Romeo and Juliet* to Jack Kerouac's "October In the Railroad Earth" to *Good Morning Vietnam* to "Bolero" to Vivaldi. James Logan High School went from *Mission Impossible* to the tango with *Zero Hour* to a timeline of American music in *The Art of Noise*, to *Carmina Burana*, to a show about boxing to a re-envisioned *Carmen* followed by *Loganation* (marches) to a show inspired by the Mythology of Odin. The Blue Devils winter guards from 1995 to 1998 offered the symphonic jazz music of Mingus to *Summertimez*, continuing with a take on *Alice in Wonderland* to the epic piano music of Rachmaninoff. The ability of the top groups to present multifaceted, dimensional competitive programs year after year often showcases an incredible amount of training and versatility. The training and versatility is indicative of the performers and the design team as well as the technical staff. A body of work that tackles a new hypothesis from season to season is a testament to the promise of successful collaboration. It's also fun.

Quite often, there can be too many cooks in the kitchen. With any collaborative process it's easy to get caught in a firing range of ideas, opinions, and philosophy. I learned quickly to simplify the process as much as possible. Defining the roles and the pathway of ideas and opinions has made for a more efficient and productive endeavor. I welcome ideas, often soliciting them, but with intense scheduling, there is simply not enough time to devote to hearing them all. It's impossible. The filtering process hopefully frees everyone to do his or her job and direct his or her energies. And I've told the overeager staff member on more than one occasion, enjoy the responsibility you have now, no matter how limited you perceive it to be. Before you know it, you could be in a different position requiring your absolute attention to multiple areas that will quickly make you long for the days when your focus was simpler. *"All in good time, my friend, all in good time."* Sometimes I long for those days where my only concern was one tiny piece of the puzzle. Especially when it's easy to be all too aware of those who are displeased with the result. I have certainly learned to simplify the chain of creative process with The Blue Devils Drum Corps. The Blue Devils have a large, highly capable staff, but focusing the developmental process through a music coordinator, Dave Glyde, and a visual coordinator, Jay Murphy, has enabled us to simplify and hopefully work more efficiently. I have depended on the talents and knowledge of John Bradford to guide the brass and percussion throughout their physical process. The chain of communication works in a trickle-down process and collaboration becomes less chaotic and more streamlined. It also helps me survive the frenzied mix of coordination and choreography.

I'm grateful for collaboration, in whatever way, shape, or form it may come. I have worked with and continue to work with brilliant people. These are people who do their jobs really well. Let them do their jobs. Find those minds that you click with and treasure the moments of not knowing. I've learned to remain open to inspiration and let the concept answer my questions. Remember, there must be an ultimate road map or vision. And always remember, the possibility of fun does exist.

CHAPTER 13

Ideas

Everyone needs ideas. It can be the most problematic and doubtful part of starting a new season. And the more people you are collaborating with the more you are defined by the schedule. I've experienced the disparity of having no idea whatsoever to the acute awareness that there were a multitude of people waiting to get started based on my decisions. Different mediums often come with different rules. And even though I'm a strong advocate of workshopping ideas, sometimes it just doesn't work out that way when it comes to the concept of a program or the thematic approach. The "big picture" idea is different from the universe of little ideas that makes a complete program. In winter guard, especially at the Raiders, we had a couple of those years where we worked on several different programs before deciding on one to pursue and complete. Drum corps, with its large creative team, snowballing calendar, and a multitude of performers, doesn't allow much freedom when it comes to deciding on the concept. So I have taken to working out upcoming themes and concepts while current competitive seasons are underway. With drum and bugle corps, I'd like to say that I'm usually a year ahead. It doesn't always work out that way, but it has been quite possible and has served us well when we are on track. I'm speaking specifically about The Blue Devils.

When I first spoke with Jay Murphy about taking on the responsibility of program coordinator he was supportive, but also stated: "Well, you better come up with a good show." *Yikes.* Cut to one of those old silent films where boiling, hot liquid is being poured from the highest walls of a castle onto the people below. He swears he didn't mean it that way, but I was nervous, apprehensive, and immediately figured out that the big idea, or concept, would be definitively important. So I probably heard it that way and exaggerated. Who knows? Add to the fact that we're talking about THE Blue Devils, too. Even if the main idea is to have no concept at all then that has perhaps become the concept. The idea can be literal, abstract, mysterious or obvious, on the nose or in the brain, emotionally servile or manipulative. The idea could simply be to display stylistic choice. The idea might be to educate, or challenge, or merely have a bit of fun. The idea can be minimalistic or complex and layered. Just writing these words is exhausting to me because there are endless combinations and possibilities. The point is that even though I might even try to deny it, I am working with a big idea, a big concept. Even if it's a non-descript or an indistinct feeling, there is something there intensely driving the project. There is something present and yearning to be experienced. Some strange motivation that suddenly becomes the "why" to the impending "how" of bringing it all to life.

Concepts can come from anywhere. And often they can come from any one person, too. Some years with The Blue Devils have started as simple conversations brainstorming the possibilities of drum and bugle corps. The mirror props from 2010 were certainly an example of a conversation on what the reality and metaphor of reflection could produce. Newsworthy events or historical perspectives can be communicated through music and motion. Poems, art, fashion, and notable people have driven the birth of a concept. A piece of music or a dance performance can grow into a reinterpreted experience. However, no matter what the idea, I am obligated to be responsible for the final decision when it comes to concept. Nothing is worse than completing a season with a group of people all pointing fingers at one another. It certainly doesn't have to be my idea and I hear a lot of pitches for show ideas. I think the people I work with appreciate decisiveness so the sooner I can provide answers the better. Now mind you, sometimes I am wrong. Seriously wrong. I hope I am learning from the failures and able to not repeat mistakes. It's the same thing we ask of performers. I have learned to ask a few questions when it comes to deciding on a concept. Sometimes I am able to academically answer and other times it's a simple feeling that an idea will work. Often I can play out the idea in my head, imagining a big idea in all its glory while I fight off insomnia during a worrysome night. Essentially all shows start with some kind of question. It may be simple questions like: "What would happen if we used a hundred vertical poles on the field?" Or it could be a little more complicated: "How can a drum corps use objects to produce multiple graphics in a variety of settings?" It could be the idea of reimagining a piece of music that has already been done or just the desire to do something melodic and upbeat. And if you want to put a Blue Devil show to that last question? The answer is Burt Bacharach. Successful or not, anytime I have worked on a project, I've realized that we are stating a hypothesis, be it simple or complex, that must in some way be explained or answered by the end.

Let's look at some crucial questions to deciding if an idea can be a concept.

1. Will the concept serve the performers?
2. Will the concept inspire the creative team to do their best work?
3. Will the concept work on multiple levels?
4. Will it provide some kind of reward for the audience?
5. Is it relevant? Is this the right time?
6. Do you care about it?
7. Can we financially afford it?

Some concepts, we have all discovered, are not meant for the short allowance of competitive time. It's difficult to try and showcase a complete biographical depiction of someone's life. There are also some figures that don't deserve to be capsulated into five or ten minutes. You have to tread carefully. The same consideration has to be given to moments in history. You have to proceed with humility and caution; making the priority of the program one of respect, justice, and service to those involved. Which takes us to...the concept eliciting the <u>appropriate</u> audience response.

I've never enjoyed or responded well to programs that were so emotionally manipulative that cause you to feel guilty if you don't react like everyone around you.

It's difficult to observe a performance about kidnapped or abused children, complete with narration and an emotional soundtrack, while the audience applauds, hollers, or whistles for the various tosses and skills being presented. Show concepts can quickly devolve into presentations that undermine the very importance of the original concept.

There are also those concepts or ideas that simply need to be put on a shelf somewhere or tucked away to gestate. Sometimes the performers are not ready to perform that "dream show" you've always wanted to do. And the same can probably be said for skills and choreography. The performers have to be trained, aware, and capable of fulfilling the intent of any given idea or you really are doing a disservice to their talent. Magic happens when the training, skill level, and maturity of the performers meets that great idea. No amount of push, pull, or force will get that circle of an idea through a square hole.

I keep a running list of show ideas and concepts. I have piles of photos, articles, magazine and newspaper clippings that might be possible ideas. I endlessly jot down ideas or keep notes on the iPhone or iPad. You never know when you're going to want to scour the gold mine of possibilities. You also never know when the timing is going to be right for a concept or idea to be translated into a program. It's best to think early and often about the upcoming opportunity and better yet, be aware of what is going on the world around you. Being relevant or finding the currency in relativity can benefit the understanding for everyone involved as well as the audience.

Unfortunately, the best intentions don't always translate. It happens to everyone. And the more people involved in the collaboration, the more it requires deciphering everyone's ability to be inspired by the idea. It's like assembling the pieces of an ideological puzzle; all it takes is one uncompromising shape to alter the outcome of the big picture. I was absolutely positive that the idea of a dance marathon would translate from the James

Logan winter guard to the Blue Devils Drum and Bugle Corps without issue.

In college we had been exposed to Twyla Tharp's incredible works including the dance piece, *Sue's Leg*. The work took a cue from the old dance marathons, hours of exhaustion, desperate and downtrodden souls pushing to the bitter edge of physical possibility for a meager prize, and the amusement of others. *It sounds a little like drum corps right?* I thought the parallels were evident and after more research, found it an interesting case of character and history. Musically, the era in our history has always intrigued me. The Depression, with its landscape of hopelessness amid a constant compulsion to move forward, was classic Americana storyline. I spoke with my father at length about his accounts of that time and I studied the movie *They Shoot Horses Don't They?* I read book after book, listened to music that could convey the tone and experimented with concepts of motion and movement.

With James Logan's world guard, the idea of how to translate all the characters and possibilities into a color guard show seemed a perfect fit. The problem I encountered was the fact that in reality the dance marathon comes to completion at its lowest physical point. The fatigue and bottomed-out depth of misery and exhaustion makes for a finale of utter doom. It was the complete antithesis to the building blocks of energy that would showcase the robust performers and their specific needs. It was Jay who mentioned the thought of moving the clock in reverse. Beginning the show at the end and taking the traumatic journey through time backwards ultimately arriving at the most energetic part of the marathon's start. I immediately liked the idea. And it fit the energy of the Logan performers. Their portrayal, accompanied by narration would be explanation and informative enough to offer a view at these heroic events. It also gave a gradation of expressive components and an opportunity to filter the idea through the window of now. Those performers were gifted at showcasing not only a variety of stylistic influences, but also at physically explaining the efforts from exhaustion to full energy.

I have never analyzed the Blue Devil's 2005 version of the show. Something about that particular incarnation of the concept didn't feel totally in place for whatever reason. The show was well received in Europe and it had its share of achievement and excellence through the skilled performers, but it was a puzzle with a few unfit parts. However, I can say that it led me to the affirmation that the disease of dictatorial impulse never belonged in the collaborative decision making process. Surely all the creative players had agreed to the idea, but I'm not so sure that I had paid enough attention to their ability to be <u>inspired</u> by the idea or not. I think it changed the fact that I would always want to see the light bulbs of imagination going off in the minds of the design team at the very mention of an idea. If a concept triggers response and sparks momentum with the design team then it is worth pursuing. Then one can at least begin to ask the other questions and clarify the validity of possibility. Reading other people's reactions is not easy. Sometimes their enthusiasm is quite visceral and obvious. At other times it takes a bit of sinking in and thoughtfulness. Knowing how to be alert to the indications takes practice, patience, and a healthy relationship with coworkers. It gets easier when working with people throughout the years and getting to know them well for sure. As much as I am concerned about providing opportunity for the performers to do their best work I also have to be just as concerned about the creative team's well-being and inclinations. Everyone wants to be presented in the very best light possible. There's nothing better than an idea that begins a chain reaction of passionate potential. And I often like to start those discussions a year or more in advance.

The Blue Devil's 2010 show *Through a Glass Darkly* was certainly motivated by Stan Kenton's incredible *City of Glass*. Karl Lowe had used the music with the Fantasia winter guard (Riverside Community College) to an astounding artistic result. (On a personal note, it was another example of how the marching and performance arts have introduced me, time and time again, to new music and thus to a new spectator experience.) The first time I saw Fantasia I immediately thought that BD could play the music and present it in an innovative, challenging manner. Interestingly enough, Karl told me he had thought the same thing. It wasn't until our discussion of the mirror props during the 2009 summer tour that the idea began to fall into place musically and visually. Those discussions, often while driving down the road, go long into the night and consist of interesting speculations of "what if" and "why not." Those conversations are never a time for throwing water on the fire; they're for fueling the embers and then taking the time to let the flames rise. Those moments are exercises in flights of fancy, entertaining, and fun. There is complete freedom.

Certainly I grew up in a time, however misguided, of corrections and stifling comments that often told me to stop acting so "silly" or to stop being so "weird." My imagination was my refuge and my fuel. The damages of inhibiting imagination, especially in children, are often our society's tether. It would be a notion that I still have to overcome and work beyond. But the sooner we encourage creativity, no matter what the discipline, the sooner we can all move forward, right? And ideas can often be born out of total flights of fancy.

And now a story about affirmation…

I am neither wholly scientific in my beliefs nor fanatical in some sort of paranormal whimsy, but I easily ricochet between the two in a state of interest. I hope that the magical exists. I desire the metaphysical. I'm an optimist. I'm hopeful even through my understanding of the alternative. So it's no surprise that I look for a sign when it comes to the situation of a new project that I am on the right track. Through the intimidation of a new venture, searching for some sign of comfort has often accompanied the long list of considerations. The sign can come from anywhere, but of course the more it produces goose bumps and a tingling of the spine all the better.

My father passed away in 2003 and we found ourselves going through the requisite cleaning of our family home. It was emotional and another rite of passage that holds a commonality for so many people. One of the many items that I really wanted to bring home to California was one of my father's Bibles. I came back home and placed the Bible on a shelf in my home office where I could see it every day. It stayed there, with a variety of mementos throughout the house, periodically being taken down for a brief moment of memory.

In the autumn of 2009 I was deep in the search for a title for the upcoming 2010 Blue Devils' program. I often look for related materials that might harken to the concept and help to define it in a curious and thought-provoking manner. I was looking through quotes about mirrors when I stumbled upon a well-known quote from the Bible.

1 Corinthians 13:12
King James Version (KJV)

[12] For now we see through a glass, darkly; but then face-to-face: now I know in part; but then shall I know even as also I am known.

I had found the Bergman 1961 film of the same title *Through A Glass Darkly* and various times throughout history where the verse had been used in a multitude of forms. I was aware of the fact that mirrors had historically often been referred to as glass. From art to music to literature the verse had been quoted or expanded upon, yet still it prompted me take my father's Bible from its place on the shelf. I wanted to see it for myself.

From the top of the Bible I could see a laminated bookmark barely rising above the worn pages. Someone, perhaps from the funeral home, had given us a copy of my father's obituary. Vital statistics of my father's life and family were written there as well as information about the funeral services as they were published in the local newspaper. I took a seat at my desk and opened the Bible to the place where the bookmark resided. I took a moment, reading the words of the obituary again and in a way pondering the fact that time had passed so quickly. The bookmark, not so much a reminder of my father himself, but of that time and those difficult days of saying good-bye. I thought about my last moment with my father.

One evening I was leaving the hospital to head to the house for some dinner when I realized that I had forgotten my coat in my dad's room. I rushed back in, letting him know I would be back in a just a bit. I told him that I loved him. I exited the hospital into the cold Georgia air and headed to the house I had called home for so long. I wasn't there for long, standing by the front door of the house when the phone rang. My niece was calling to tell me to get back to the hospital. I automatically knew the circumstance. I could tell it in her voice. I made my way to the inevitable. He was gone.

The flash of this memory returned while I glanced over the coated bookmark. Then I looked down to see what page had been marked by its placement in the bible. It was First Corinthians and I found the exact verse. *OK, cue The Twilight Zone music now.* Whatever the coincidence, the happenstance, or the sheer accident of the occurrence might be, I took it as a sign. People really never leave us do they? And, what could be considered a silly little search for the title of a drum corps show was a moment I cannot and will not forget.

The impetus not only for the *Casablanca* show, but also for *The Godfather* show was the striking, recognizable, memorable melody that each one of those movie soundtracks offered. A simple melody can prompt the whirlwind of ideas that form development, choreography, and character and evolve into a fully realized production. Logan's boxing show was a germ of an idea after I had seen a competitive dance team present their own unique version. The question of how each generation of young people relates to the world of musical marches prompted *Loganation*. Musical motivation meets current street-smart style.

The 2008 Blue Devils interpretation of Ferlinghetti's *Constantly Risking Absurdity* came from my love for the St. Anthony's winter guard and their classic, iconic style as well as the question of bringing a poem to life on a football field. Creative risks certainly paralleled the designer and performers' experience so the poem was a relevant opportunity for metaphor. The 2009 program entitled *1930* started as a question of taking one year in history and examining it's highlights, music, tone, and cultural ether. The number one song of the year 1930 was "Happy Days Are Here Again," something the Blue Devils had previously performed and a show that I, as a fan, loved. That was a sign. That seminal tune is a Blue Devils standard used beautifully in 1988.

In 1996 I decided to test out my yearning to create a show based on railroads. I was with the wonderful performers and staff at Beyer High School in Modesto, California. On a trip home for the holidays I sat with my father and used a rickety old cassette recorder to record his stories of trains and childhood. I incorporated his voice into the soundtrack and I'm glad I have that chance to watch the energetic performers and hear his voice. I revisit that show often just to hear him.

The idea ignites and the research begins. Even within concepts that might simply be studies in style or approach, the fleshing out of the many layers that exist with any idea or motivation become an integral part of the process. Even through a simple pop song the possibility of discovering the archeological inner workings provide myriad thoughts and emotional narrative. Whether or not the audience needs to understand every layer of depth and thought, it still exists. The stratum is there for the taking by anyone willing to be open to its revelation. And hopefully a good idea becomes a wonderful program that can be viewed time and time again. The thought of people wanting to see a show again is exciting to me and should make promoters ecstatic.

For me, the idea is to pay attention to all that surrounds me. Ideas will whisper to me, shout or jump at me from any direction. They leap from the pages of history or literature. They urge me to tap a foot or move around my hotel room. They jog a memory and give me chills or they silently linger until a crystal clear image appears. They can strike from moments of improvisation. They can be simple or multilayered. They can be overt or impressionistic. They can rise from a single word or an epic poem. A spark emerges. The work begins.

CHAPTER 14

Felliniesque

The 2014 Blue Devils program is an unexpected tale. If I had the wherewithal, this would be the sixteenth chapter for obvious reasons. This show would mark the sixteenth Championship title for the Blue Devils.

Following 2013 and *The Re:Rite of Spring*, not exactly popular fare for many, my thoughts were leaning to something lighter, perhaps with more sense of whimsy, and hopefully, beauty in the traditional sense of the word, as well as fun. It would be the word that Dave Gibbs, like any good director/producer would charge, kept offering as motivation as I discussed ideas, concepts, and format with Dave Glyde and Jay Murphy. Make it fun. Make it fun. It was virtuous direction. Granted, I had thought all the ideas were fun in the past, but I understood the baseline tone of the note. Drum corps is a different animal and it has tendencies to elicit strong reactions and opinions. I get it. *The Re:Rite of Spring*, which I still have a very strong, positive and proud affection for, was done for a specific time and the anniversary of its debut which, like it or not, was monumental. It's an important, influential work not unlike the strength of conviction I carried for Kenton's *City of Glass*. For quite some time The Blue Devils have been trying to offer contrast from program to program or season to season. Often my best example for people is to remind them of the World Guard's ricochet from Mingus (1995) to the wonderful pop melody of "Summertime" (1996). So the plan was never to follow Stravinsky with something the same or even similar. And many people, without reflecting on our previous pattern, were quick to warn me of following Stravinsky with something of the same persuasion. It was never my intention and I'm sure it wasn't Jay or Dave Glyde's either. We like the adventure of something different and new. From Bacharach to "Happy Days Are Here Again," all the shows have reasons to their timing.

As always I scoured my notes during the summer of 2013 searching for what might be a left turn for the upcoming season. It's a good time amid the intensity of one competitive season to exercise some liberty and imagine another direction. Several ideas were rising to the top, which I would carefully toss into conversations with Jay or Dave Glyde. I won't mention any of those ideas here because they may awaken from their sleepiness at some point demanding to be performed. There was one idea in particular that kept returning to the forefront and had it not been for copyright restrictions would have probably been the 2014 program. The final verdict came down in the fall and Dave, Jay and I made our way to Dave Gibb's home for a meeting. Tossing the possible replacement concepts around was like throwing pasta at the wall waiting to see if it would stick. Nothing seemed to resonate.

And I'll be the first to admit that I was bruised from the 2013 season. So many people had such strong reactions one way or the other that I found it confusing. More so than any other year, 2013 had left me feeling a bit unable to please, yet absolutely sure of our strength at fulfilling a concept. I was sure that we could bring life to a concept, and I was resolute in the talent of the performers. I wasn't confident in the fact that every audience would be willing to take the ride with us. Once again, that age-old desire to please people would return. It always does regardless of what naysayers might like to make you believe. We care deeply. Sometimes it seems damn near impossible to please everyone involved and the weight of that concern followed me into the autumn months.

We spent hours mulling over thoughts and potential concepts with the typical detours into a variety of other subjects. The word "beautiful" had been in my head since the previous summer and I could not wrap my head around what it meant. Mainly because I had thought all the shows were beautiful in their own way. It's always been a bit of mantra for me that no matter how dark a show might be that it could still possess a sense of beauty. Anytime I had veered in an unfortunate direction I usually felt like it was my lack of attention to that very edict: Take an idea and make it a thing of beauty. Finally, we decided to depart the hamster wheel of our meeting and convene again at a later time.

In the driveway of Dave Gibb's house, Dave, Jay and I sat on the ground for one last recap. For a few more minutes we were tossing and turning the desperation over and over from subject to subject that seemed to lead nowhere. Somehow we made our way to Fellini. It was something I had talked about ever since the 2006 *Godfather* show. Listen to enough Nino Rota music, and it's easy to realize the amount of depth, drama, and yes, beauty, to his incredible body of work. And after researching Rota's work, it inevitably leads to Fellini's movies. So here was an idea that had been in the ether since 2006 that waited patiently for the right time, the right device, and our awakening to its potency, both musically and visually.

For the three of us I think it only took our respective drives home that night to begin to connect all the dots. For me I had spent years enamored, and yes, a bit obsessed with the Broadway musical *Nine*, Based on Fellini's *8½*, *Nine* dealt with a biographical stratosphere as well as the creative process. I can't tell you how many summers I spent listening to "Guido's Song." Every lyric of the song provided a brief explanation of my own exaggerated, yet authentic sense of process. The real question would be whether or not, or how, we could conjure even a speck of Fellini's essence for a drum corps audience. For me the connection was cinema in general. *Everyone can relate to movies, right?* So, even if an audience had no idea of the iconic Fellini, they might be able to enjoy the imagery of cinema. It would be a risk, but what else is new? It seemed a good as time as any to venture into the Maestro's world.

Then the research process began with an abundance of viewing Fellini's work. I watched Fellini movies constantly. I read everything I could. I rummaged through countless clips on YouTube. I watched interview after interview. I re-watched such musicals as *Sweet Charity*, which was based on a Fellini film. I listened and listened to soundtracks and scores. I started to conjure a method of moving in small moments of improvisation at home or while traveling. A hip leads. A head turns. A shoulder rolls into a slow motion reach. While you ride in the airport shuttle or enter a movie theatre, flashes of imagery start to appear. Hopefully the entire process would imprint itself into my thoughts and actions.

I can't even pretend to define Federico Fellini academically. I'll let you do that research for yourself, but needless to say, this man was a giant of the film world.

The show began to fall easily into an organized three-act exploration. Religion, the circus, and sensuality were thematically definitive aspects of Fellini's life and work. All the while I was sure that even if the viewer never understood this motivation; the idea of a movie set with it's props and assortment of characters could provide a level of understanding and yes, enjoyment. The landscape of Fellini's world was a soundstage and it seemed appropriate to let that idea become the setting for the show. Originally, my feeling was of stark minimalism and a strong contrast to a hundred poles for *The Re:Rite of Spring*. An image had lodged itself into my psyche during the 2013 summer: an incredibly long elevated runway of mobile platforms that could be used in a variety of ways and shapes. Once the Fellini idea came into focus, I could see a camera at the end of the runway. The image was fixed in my head. It was Jay who kept insisting on a multitude of props of varying size and shape. I'm glad he did. Once the setting was established, those different objects would continue to provide variety, opportunity, and surprise. The props would be things you might actually see on a sound stage. The props also gave Jay a variety of ways to stage the corps and present vignettes, scenes, and action. The importance of not looking like anyone else would again be paramount. It made total sense and I simply had to release my paranoia and move forward. For many years I've stuck with the color white for props mainly because of the ever-present white lines on football fields. It's another idea that's perpetually ingrained and I hope I can let it go at some point. But it would serve a ghostly, magical effect in a show superimposed onto an imaginary movie set. And I was pleased at how Dave Gibbs was also insistent on the need to really go "full out" if we were going to take on the concept of Fellini. He never hesitated even when I was on a merry-go-round of insecurity.

I always have certain ideas on what music is essential for certain concepts and this year would not be different. I was also adamant about the tambourine-yielding dancers from "Be Italian" in the musical *Nine*. There are snippets of musical moments that play out in my head and I can visualize them complete with costumes and choreography. Often, I cannot fully explain how they work, how they fit, or how they are constructed, but I can "feel" them and Dave Glyde is, more often than not, a good sport when it comes to my insistent whims. Dave began his research process also and was bringing incredible musical ideas to the table. My trust in him, as always, was absolute. He's also a good sport about letting me edit or ask for rewrites. It was Dave who would offer the idea to have the composer Gordon Goodwin write something original for the corps. At the time, I wasn't familiar with the Grammy-award winning Mr. Goodwin (something that I'm not proud of now that I've heard his work). *There's still so much to learn; still so much to know.* But here was one of those moments that Dave Glyde was so sure of himself that I knew to trust his instincts. I've learned that you have to know when to release your own opinions or limitations and have faith in the people who are there to do a job. And as Dave Gibbs let me know, it was a lot of money for our non-profit to pay for commissioning an original piece of music. Budget constraints are ever present and this would be no exception. I kept trusting and hoping for the best.

Creating and designing the show would be a lengthy process well into the time when the members would be moved into the area for what are called "all-days." But barely into the first steps of our discovery it would be time to come up with a title. For the longest time the title of the show was *Fellini's Ghost*. That's what it was for me day after day. I took it as a sign when I opened an issue of *Vanity Fair* magazine to see a sidebar article with that very title. I snapped a photo of the page and kept it on my phone for the longest time. It made sense to me that in the act of honoring this icon that we could only hope that his presence would be felt; a haunting, metaphysical watchdog over our endeavor. The show title didn't change until it was time to put together a write-up that could be used for publicity. Sometimes show titles are challenging for announcers and I understand that. *Constantly Risking Absurdity* in 2008 comes to mind: the word "absurdity" devolving into the mispronounced "absur-vity." So I certainly wasn't sure that the word "ghost" would be understood as singular or plural. Furthermore, I wasn't sure that "ghost" shouldn't be plural following the idea of the cast of characters that inhabited Fellini's films. Either way, "ghost" is like the word "breast" or "quest" or "risk" where the plural ends up sounding like a hissing snake—and who knows what would happen when it's announced over a sound system in a huge arena. The echo of a mispronunciation could make that into one uninvitingly large reptile. "Ghosts-sssssss."

When you read about Fellini the word Felliniesque is a relevant description that has become a part of the lexicon. It means the fantastical or surreal and "in the manner of" the films of the maestro Federico Fellini. I liked the way it rolled off the tongue. It also gave us license to move beyond the literal and create something from our own point of view. I ran my indecision by Jay and Dave Gibbs both and they were quick to answer that the word "Felliniesque" was the right choice. It would be another good sign that they didn't hesitate and it was just the confirmation I needed. We were off and running and soon I would begin the write-up for the show. This is worth mentioning because it was presented in the format of a film script, albeit with some creative license. But it shows that finding a way to keep the concept ever present, through every detail possible, is vital. It becomes a part of everything we do, and it quickly gets into our bloodstream, our thoughts, and, ultimately, our actions. And I liked the thought of the consistency. This is a good place to mention that I like to have my work checked by people I trust. The mock script of a write-up was sent to Michael Zapanta. Zap is a professional in the film industry who spearheads (and has innovated) the exceptional media work that the Blue Devils have presented. Zap presented me with corrections and suggestions and offered to spend some time talking with me about the show. It was a great opportunity. We sat on a rickety wooden bench behind a local Starbucks and spent a while on an array of cinematic subjects. At one point it even veered into my own insecurities on pleasing audiences, having artistic integrity, and deflecting the negativity that can sometimes pervade our drum corps community. Zap was quick to point out that even the most experienced professionals have these concerns. Who knows if a film will succeed? Do you go for big box office or make that independent passion project? Do you do what you feel is important to you or do you ignore your own instincts to speculate on what might be important to another portion of audience? How do you find the balance? In the end it was eye-opening for me to know that even the most successful of folks might have the same anxiety. The conversation with Zap might as well have been a therapy session with me horizontal on the bench while he took notes on a legal pad. It helped me and it was another means by which to move ahead. *Thanks, Zap.* It's an odd conundrum that I feel totally responsible when things don't please certain people, but barely responsible when they do. *Weird, huh? It might be time for that therapist appointment after all.*

My resident mental image of the long white runway remained as we began the design process. I knew that the show should open with a solo dancer making his or her way to a waiting camera. The part went to our beautiful color guard captain Samantha Madayag. She reached the camera that ignited the sound of a projector signaling the motion of the narrative. I love metaphors and quite often the metaphor is the test to determine whether a moment is correct, in the right place, or conceptually appropriate. I also like twisting the logic of a given moment shattering what might be realistic expectation. The camera initiating the sound of a projector is one of those moments that jumped realism, but had a logical connection of action/result. They are inevitably related, but the camera doesn't make the same sound as a projector. I liked the twist. Jay used the imagery of the spinning film reels to begin the upcoming cinematic fanfare and the spin of the reels would become a motif for the show. It's virtually impossible to get one of the classic movie fanfares for use in drum corps, but I loved Dave Glyde's idea to use forty trumpets. The parallel of the triumphant announcement to the religious grandeur seemed perfect and grand.

Beyond quite literal references such as the white tops on the dancers with their ceremonial uniformity, there were those moments that expressed emotional aspects of spirituality. The mountain of film flags like a pyramid reaching upward to a group of young men with sabers maneuvering the runway like a gauntlet while musicians rolled, jumped, or crawled across the white pathway were symbolic evidence of religious exploration. It's OK for me when people don't get it all. Honestly, I know sometimes I've been too vague. But the result is ultimately what matters and I enjoy the layers that people can discover or simply enjoy and not really know, or care, exactly why. I have those same moments as an audience member from Mark Morris to Cirque; I love the experience in all its layers and potential for enlightenment.

We would begin with the color guard on all saber. Sabers were an obvious choice for the guard because for me they looked like how those forty trumpets sounded—sparkling, glistening, silver-notes reflecting light. The corps could take on roles that ranged from crew and stagehands to the all-too-human pull and struggle of life, love, and death. I even described the departure of the guard making their way to the heap of props as the quick-paced shuffle of nuns scurrying through the Italian street. Fellini, and this show, would prove to make metaphor, symbolism, and imagination the central mode of operation. If the thought could occur it was just as logical that it could be seen—all leading to an emotional and visual stream of consciousness.

La Strada means "the road" in Italian, which led to the long white runway placed front and center with another character laboring the length, literally and emotionally. The *La Strada* theme is beautiful to me and it was a "moment" when I heard the horn line play it for the first time. After hearing the ballad I knew this could be a competitively viable program and I stated as such to Jay and Dave. The ballad would open the door to Fellini's circus realm. For me, it was a theme of rescue and needed to do nothing more than present that idea. I was glad that Jay agreed. It would have been a lost moment had we tried to frantically speed our way through it with drill and too much motion. Patrick Griggs, a veteran, would take on the role of what I called the "broken clown" or "string-less puppet." I improvised the long haul of the runway a few times and then Patrick began to make it his own. It was perfect. The emotional moment would have to be real and authentic, and not about perfectly imitating me. Loette Snead, one of our stunning female performers with her statuesque height would follow Patrick with an exaggerated umbrella. Another symbol of protection and rescue that she could finally, at the trek's end, shelter Patrick and give him emotional rescue. The ballad was always an emotional statement. Anyone can relate to that desire for protection or rescue and it was never meant to be anything else. The choreography dealt in support, reaction, and rebounded moments that finally brought everyone to the main character offering support through his struggle. A couple of times it would be brought to my attention that I had, through the choreography and concept, mocked a state of disability. Even one judge was vocal about it being offensive. Nothing could have been further from the truth and it had never crossed my mind to perceive it in such a way. I hoped it wasn't an indication of controversy to come and yet I strongly believed in the theme of rescue, protection, and support. And I believed in the validity that such a statement could exist in a Felliniesque moment. I still resolve that it was an emotional statement manifested through physical movement.

The Gordon Goodwin music, with its Blue Devil flair, fit perfectly into the circus section of the show. Complete with a circus ring full of daring performers to dancing girls, Fellini's childhood infatuation with the carnival-like existence could parallel our drum corps summer. As we worked on the production Jay and I sat in the "office" (which was my car parked alongside the rehearsal field). My car would become a quiet place to observe the action and still speak openly and honestly in private. It was in my car one day, as we watched a run-through of the previous work being performed that I said to Jay,

"If my name was Karl Lowe I would have someone tossing rifles into the symbolic circus ring from the top of one of the taller props."

Karl is a master of those high-flying moments that I'm frequently apprehensive about adding into a show. I'm lucky that Karl consults and helps counsel me through the process at the Blue Devils. Jay of course told me that I should try it. One of the guys, Cody Newill, seemed perfectly confident for such a risky moment and proved my assumption right throughout the summer, show after show. It would be another circus-like moment and Cody was a great example of how giving the right information on character and motivation could free them to instill their own nuance to the scene. Watch Cody on the top of the prop and you'll see a developed character full of physicality, gesture, showmanship, and completeness.

The girls got to perform with rhythmic gymnastic ribbons throughout this production also. I liked the metaphor of a lion tamer and the fact that the ribbons were digitally printed as film frames. In fact, all the flags in the show were versions of film frame with the last set of flags containing the words "The End."

The last part of the show would allude to the sensual, and yes, sexual aspect of Fellini movies. Watch the "Be Italian" production from *Nine* and you'll understand the necessity for such a reference. Again, there would be those people who thought it went too far and I was glad that I had discussed the issue early on with guard. It was never choreographed to the extent of what audiences can see from cheerleaders, dancers on television, or those beauty pageants for children. Yet it was inevitable that it would be considered too risqué for some and I was satisfied with that early in the process. It was an important part of the show and a statement that needed to be made. I never felt like it crossed the line into inappropriateness and fortunately I was supported by the powers that be, and yes, our college-aged performers.

As the show progressed to the end the whirlwind of film references would begin to come together almost as a fast edit process. This included one scene with snare drummers on a makeshift stage surrounded by the girls for what I liked to call the "table read." Samantha stood atop one of the ladders with a feather fan while the corps produced a long diagonal. I loved how Jay lined the diagonal up so that the ladder had a spot. It's part of what I admire about his brilliance in thinking the process of form could marry the existence of props on a field of a hundred yards. It's an enormous canvas in which every object present plays a part in the overall picture and every thing is a character. The finale of the show was about the image of film encompassing the field and turning the camera, a major player in the show, on the audience. I liked the idea that it let the audience know that they were a part of the show, too.

Felliniesque

The summer began strong and the show was being well received. On more that one occasion people would comment to me that they assumed we would be making a bold statement after finishing in second place in 2013. Some even went so far as to say that they knew we would be "mad" (as in angry) after losing the previous season and would come back strong. This was perplexing to me because first of all, I wasn't mad about losing in 2013 and secondly, I never thought the show would play like an act of vengeance. Maybe some people can, but it's impossible for me to create out of anger. It's not productive and it's not fun. Now I can be paranoid and I was absolutely sure that I would spend the first two weeks of shows crawling on the floor of a dirty RV looking for my self-esteem. But the creative process for me has to be fun, and anger just leaves me miserable and drained. Remember, I know that losing is not the end of the world unless it really is the last time competing and even then I know that I should probably have some perspective. It's got to be about the work. It's got to be about the body of work. Things can change from year to year quite drastically. I've learned to enjoy the moments while I can, wherever they might be.

2014 would be one of those memorable years from a creative and a competitive standpoint. For the most part, audiences came along for the ride whole-heartedly with *Felliniesque*, which was a "win" in and of itself regardless of the score. Performers and staff members from other corps were gracious. Adjudicators acknowledged the work. Championships ended with a first place, a record high score, and a wonderful response. There were monumental caption wins that included a seventh consecutive first place for the color guard. I never assumed it would happen and I never expected it to happen. The summer was about the performers and the show. Even in that last week I knew that anything could happen and the Blue Devils have plenty of years of proof that another drum corps could suddenly emerge competitively. *It ain't over til it's over.* And it was worth it.

Champions perform an encore after winning in a much more relaxed atmosphere. I love encores without that pressure and anxiety of the competitive moment. I love the audience that stays for the encore. I watch each and every moment of the show, remembering when and where they were created and taught. I can recall tiny details such as where I was standing in my backyard as Dave Glyde pitched the idea of using forty trumpets. I can remember listening to him on my phone and looking at a particularly green row of ivy growing alongside the patio. I flashback to a winter guard show where I asked Blue Devil icon Shirley Dorritee if she thought I could bring back the ribbons only this time as film frames. I recall the day that our set-engineer Jon Burroughs delivered the various props. I watch performers flawlessly execute those skills that might have challenged them all summer. It's emotional and it's awesome. I cry a lot! There's no other way to put it.

Felliniesque. Who knew?

CHAPTER 15

Desire Overcomes Doubt

TJ Doucette is the technical director for the Blue Devils color guard. She was the first person I heard say this phrase: Desire overcomes doubt. She probably said it with the color guard during the summer at some point. From the moment the words left her mouth it made sense to me. It has a truth to it and a rhythm as you say it. It's like some poetic line that serves as a mantra. You can recite it over and over, turning it upside down and inside out while it seeps into your system to propel you. We all have doubts. Doubts can be the tiniest of seedlings of a massive emotional redwood tree.

If you know you are different, that you hear a different drum or simply have that constant sensation of unease, you probably understand the ambition to not settle until you find complete peace of mind. *Is that even possible?* It's a desire and if you can keep propelling yourself forward, albeit with a sense of patience, you can overcome your doubt. You find yourself hanging on to whatever might further your pursuit until you can discover a new setting. Desire is key.

How many times have nerves or self-doubt gotten the better of a performer? It's easy to get lost in the reasons why a moment will NOT be successful instead of harnessing the energy and transforming it into power. But it is ultimately just that—energy. Nerves are energy. It courses through our bodies as adrenaline or self-deprecating voices. Recognizing our baseline awareness of desire can manifest a new perspective and sometimes, given the proper work and discipline, be just enough to get us through the sensation of being powerless.

For performers, being aware that desire can overcome doubt can be key to finding breath and having faith in the hours and hours spent in preparation. Knowing that one is part of something bigger than oneself is a comfort, too. You are not alone. Let the show do its work. Make your desire to be as proficient in the product as possible. Forget all the outside interference.

Where exactly does confidence come from? I wish I had the exact answer to that question. Certainly preparation provides confidence a supportive foundation. Color guard performers spend hours training movement technique. Then there are the hours spent on learning to operate and manipulate a variety of pieces of equipment. Knowing how to control your thought process while performing becomes another valuable skill: concentration. The ability to communicate through the various technical efforts becomes another layer. Hours turn into days that turn into months and years and hopefully, at the highest level, there is a divine harmony of all the considerations of technique, style, and communication.

The advancements of what young people are bringing to the table in terms of skillsets are mind boggling to me. Marching bands are now venturing into new levels of movement and dance. The simultaneous responsibility of using the body at such a high level and playing music with the same concern for excellence has become an amazing feat. Now I'm not even approaching the subject of how these color guard and marching band musicians are required to be aware of their placement within formations and their relationships to one another.

Add to all of that the fact that there is often theatrical character built into the entire process. So, basically the performers are acting, dancing, and playing all at the same time. It's a staggering thought. The training that it takes to come even close to fully realizing all these efforts is without question mentally and physically beneficial. So the next time you hear someone say, "Oh, that's just a marching band" or "That's just that color guard thing" or "That's just drums and buglers," you will know the absurdity in that person's ignorance. It's easy to proclaim us all "geeks" and "dorks." Easy. Without any research or awareness of the varying levels of participation that we encompass, it's easy to label us all based on limited knowledge of who and what we are. The unknown, no matter what the case, is always an easy mark. It's all the more reason for not only marketing and promotion on our behalf, but also for a unification of all of us, past and present, who have experienced the benefits of music and motion.

Watch the Honda Battle of the Bands sometime and you'll see an entirely unique style and approach to marching entertainment. It's another example of how diverse styles can be within the marching world. It's amazing and entertaining! Once again, the statement that something so athletic, energetic, and theatrical could be "just a marching band" is absurd and entirely incorrect. It's much, much more. Our diversity is also another reason for never, ever assuming that there is only one "real" way to practice what we are. If we were all held to the same stylistic preference, wouldn't we all look exactly the same?

I know there are studies out there that have extolled and expounded upon the physical and mental virtues of the pageantry world. Much smarter people than me have done studies and written great papers on just how music and motion can catapult the mind and body to new levels of achievement. The proof is there. It's more reason why great consideration should be taken when schools would dare to eliminate any level of marching music programs. It is scientifically, medically, and emotionally undeniable that marching arts provide value. And music education and appreciation has longevity. It is something that we can not only enjoy, but also continue to practice for as long as we live.

There are benefits in every level of participation. Every runner you see jogging on the side of the road is not an Olympic athlete. Every tennis player is not training for Wimbledon. But they are participating, and they are actively pursuing something that is beneficial to them on multiple levels. The mechanics of engagement ignite virtue and stability and confidence to the participant. So even for the hobbyist, the non-competitive individual, or the marching band that is struggling to build its membership, the benefits still exist. There are people who are not professional dancers taking dance class. There are musicians who make wonderful music simply for themselves. The virtues last a lifetime and they nurture confidence and communication. Training can give you confidence and confidence can give wings to your desires.

There is most likely a healthy side to doubt, too. I don't ever stand at the start of something new without some amount of doubt. Even after all these years I still can be tortured by the prospect of beginning again. Sometimes it's a dull ache and other times it's torturous. I hope this doubt is simply the acknowledgement that I don't know everything there is to know. The doubt really doesn't go away, and people who think they know right away when something is complete and worthy amaze me. It takes awhile for me to know when a program is good. I will question my choices or my part in the design equation to the very last performance. Even as I look back at previous shows I still question. It was Martha Graham who called it the "divine dissatisfaction." It's true. Sure, there may be parts, or pieces of the puzzle, that I feel pleased with, but there is always that slight doubt that something could have been better. Every year is different and my confidence ebbs and flows through various degrees of content. But one thing is for sure, I can never be sure. Nothing is for certain. Doubt is a hefty boulder or a tiny pebble. It simply becomes a part of the equation.

We spent a lot of my youth traveling to North Carolina to my grandparent's tobacco farm. I loved the farm and it was a welcome escape and fueled my active imagination. My mother had grown up in this area near McLeansville and the exact acreage of the land would change depending on whom you might ask. But I know that it was large and spacious with fields and woods and creeks and all kinds of animals. It was big enough that even through all the years I spent roaming the vast area I never felt like I saw it all. It was peaceful and it was beautiful and it was a safe place. I could take walks with my grandfather on dirt paths worn by the years of horse-pulled canvas tobacco bins or old tractors. I could sing at full volume while I stood on bales of hay in the loft of the barn. I could sit on moss-covered rocks by a creek or venture up a hill to pick blackberries. I could listen to the rain on the tin roof of the front porch and I could pile the homemade quilts on the bed to stay warm in the winter. I could slide down snowy hills riding an old piece of metal. My grandparent's collie, Rocky, would follow behind me as I roamed and imagined and dreamed. Rocky would be my imaginary audience as I twirled a tall tobacco stick in the middle of a plowed-over field. I was oblivious to the financial hardships of the farm and the struggles my aging grandparents faced while trying to maintain the tiny farmhouse, the barn, and a series of chicken coops. It was all magic and Rockwell to me and I wish I could have known my grandparents as an adult simply to thank them for the world they created.

That little guy twirling that tobacco stick is not that distant a memory for me. I can access his fascination and his desire. And I can certainly recall that time where doubt was not even a consideration. That's an example of what I try to access when I'm swimming in the unsure. I can see the performers' faces. I can hear the audience. I can feel the music. Sometimes you just have to stop for a second and find that feeling of freedom, take a breath and take a step.

CHAPTER 16

There's Something to Be Said for...

Winning.
I'll be the first to say that I have been fortunate to work with the best people. I have been, and continue to be, surrounded by talented, intelligent, passionate, insightful, and challenging people. They dare to ask questions and set forth to discover the answers. They are people who, in the great creative unrest, desire to constantly take the necessary steps to fulfillment. That, in and of itself, is a vibrant example of winning. One of the first things I've learned about winning is that it has many definitions. It is defined by myriad situations and circumstances. Most importantly, winning hopefully teaches us to know the difference between rationalizing our shortcomings or truly experiencing forward momentum.

Winning competitively certainly removes the albatross of that speculation. Once it happens, it is a reality that no one can take from you. No longer can you find excuses or indulge self-pity. Winning allows us to share a moment in time that is the completion of a process and enables us to join those before us who have experienced the same exclamation point. We deserve to be proud—proud of those around us and of every single person who played a part in making the reward possible. It has taken me a long time to come to terms with the fact that I own the wins as much as anyone else. The perception of bragging or boastful arrogance is something that others can easily pin on us even without cause. Simply sitting down to write these thoughts sends me into a cold sweat at the thought of how some people might perceive it all. But it's important to take those moments with our fellow champions or in a silent moment of isolation, to actually allow ourselves to embrace the results of a job well done—no matter how we define winning.

This brings to mind an important point, however. Beyond accolades, trophies, or gold medals, I have never felt as if I had defeated someone else. I can say this in all honesty after a lot of years and reflection. Competitive success for me has always been the fulfillment of the performers and the show first and foremost. This is followed by the acknowledgment that we have met the criteria of a given scoring system as applied by a panel of subjective, opinioned adjudicators. I find it difficult to perceive the pageantry arts as one person beating another. And because I've yearned for longevity from the very beginning, I always knew that things can quickly change leaving me facing an entirely different result the next time around. That being said, I've learned that it's OK to catch my breath and be grateful that I've successfully completed the task. One can appreciate the fact that one has done good work. Winning is a great achievement. Usually those who think anything less are forgetting that they entered into competition in the first place. If you don't wish to compete, which sometime I actually don't, then find another venue or avenue to communicate and produce. But, here's the hitch, there's always some degree that you will experience competitive efforts. You could be competing for a score, or a positive review from a critic, or simply for ticket sales. You might be competing for funding or the chance to showcase your art.

Winning for the Connecticut Skylarks in 1984 was my first gold medal experience at WGI. Interestingly I felt so much of that year's result as a tribute to Mickey Kelly and that particular group: it was much bigger than a personal victory. With only a few years around the Skylarks, I still felt that their contribution to the activity was monumental and I certainly was aware of what I learned from them even as a spectator. That very same year I had begun my journey with State Street, and their second-place finish was a victory also. They didn't <u>lose</u> the gold medal—they <u>won</u> the silver medal. It was also State Street's announcement that they would now be on the world championship scene. They would now be a creative and dynamic force of their own.

The first time I experienced a competitive win at DCI was 1994 with the Blue Devils. It had been a long drought for them after winning their last title in 1986. Again, it did not feel so much personal as an extraordinary recognition of the Blue Devils' ability to reinvent themselves, reach new standards of excellence and emerge with an ambitious revitalized energy. The Blue Devils, contrary to what some believe, do not preach winning. They are not in denial about the desire to win, but they certainly have proven their ability to survive losing or winning. It all comes down to achievement. I have listened from the outside to different groups preaching their philosophy of winning before or after competitions. It may come as a surprise to see how organizations can often present one public view while harboring quite the opposite. Most of them have not found themselves in a championship position. Misguided focus is the reason.

The truth of the matter is that once you pass the stereotypical "winning" scenario you begin to understand what it means to compete with yourself. Beyond the score, placements, or commentary comes the realization that it is about the individual artist moving to his or her next level. The Blue Devils did not need, in the literal sense of the word, a sixteenth title. But that number certainly represents their ability to push, consistently and with great passion, to take another step forward. Each and every one of those titles represents growth and a profound experience of achievement for those involved. And every Championship was made up of some returning participants as well as fresh faces who had never won before. Each corps or color guard was a different group with a different dynamic and desire to excel.

Winning can be quite uncomfortable, too. Winning comes with a brand new kind of attention and pressure. Suddenly the expectations exist and there is an obligation to offer something fresh to the evolution of the art. The same pressure exists for those groups who become audience favorites, too. The audience now has their own specific memory and the new charge becomes the quest to match or surpass something that resides as recollection for so many people. Sometimes it seems impossible.

After a win, I often fall right into thinking of what comes next. *What do we do now? What's the next show? Where do we go from here?* It's a colossal, overwhelming feeling that leaves little time to enjoy the moment. Perhaps it's one of the reasons I now like to have at the very least an inkling of an idea in place when the season is over. I am assured that the fluidity from one year to the next will happen minus the panic or insecurity. Win or lose, next steps are important anyway.

I enjoy watching college football. It often provides a nostalgic respite from being an adult. Southerners love their football and nothing feels more comfortable than autumn weather, comfortable sweaters, and the noise of the energetic crowd and the sounds of cheerleaders and marching band music. It's a comforting memory of my childhood. Needless to say, I'm a fan of the SEC teams. And I'm a great admirer of the great coaches, past and present. Of course I was glued to the television for the 2013 SEC West Championship game between Alabama and Auburn. It was thrilling to watch even though I wasn't even particularly invested in who would win the game. I am, however, a big admirer of Nick Saban and the Alabama program. Once again, following their loss, I was floored by negative comments I was reading online. Some of it was directed at the team and often included malicious attacks on the integrity of Saban. I began to read posts from people taking to the anonymity of their computers to voice opinions and basically use the Internet as a toilet. It's disappointing and discouraging. I couldn't understand it and maybe that's because I'm not so well versed in the details of the sport. I'm simply a fan. But given my apparent ignorance on any backstory, it certainly seemed far too intense and downright vicious at times. I did a little reading online and stumbled across an article written by sports writer Shaun Powell that I found particularly relevant.

He wrote:

One thing about this country, we don't waste our time being jealous over losers and people who don't achieve. We do find passionate

reasons to love and hate winners and also remain fascinated by them because they can do what most of us can't or won't.

Losing.

Every competitive instance provides a learning experience. There is always something to be gained even through the disappointment of a loss. It's my father's optimism once again bubbling to the surface I'm sure. But an individual's definition of losing says a lot about that person. I've also not been in a situation where my job or my livelihood depended on a win. The pressure and the desire have certainly been there, but I've never been given that directive. I think the quality of what I contribute is always evaluated and I'm fortunate to work for people who take all the various aspects of what we do into consideration.

Not finishing in first place provides information. And whether you agree with the outcome or not, there is something to be gained by looking at the experience from every angle. When the Blue Devils finished second to the Phantom Regiment in 2008, my first reaction was not anger or shock; it was first and foremost how to find the passion that I saw in Phantom's performance. I saw it and I felt it through their performance. And if you keep yourself open to the atmosphere of a summer of contests, you can often feel the swell of another show gaining momentum. I was pleased that the audience was delighted and I was happy for Phantom. I had enormous respect and admiration for the rise of Carolina Crown in 2013 and was genuinely happy for them. They uniquely and skillfully found a voice that was a sure sign of achievement. But I know how that pressure of the next step is daunting and any repeat winners can tell you how difficult those steps can be. Both Phantom and Crown created and showcased sheer brilliance, creatively and competitively; those are now cherished parts of drum corps history. I hope that wins and losses are given perspective by longevity. Longevity of excellence and achievement benefits everyone, regardless of wins or losses.

If you are in the game for the long haul, sometimes losing gives you a chance to catch your breath and reconfigure your approach. It can cause a wonderful impetus for change and embellished, reinvigorated creativity. If you can rise above the disappointment, there is a certain freedom in going back to the drawing board. Losing color guard at DCI with the Spirit of Atlanta in 1986 was certainly a disappointment. That color guard was approaching a level of professionalism that was new for drum corps and their communication skills were ground breaking. They were the real deal. But 1987 simply became about getting back in the game and getting back to work. I never, ever expected them to pull out a win that season in color guard. It wasn't the focus. They were talented, full of personality, and certainly upholding the standards of the previous year. I just didn't think it was possible and surprise, it happened.

In 1988, The Chaparrals from Tate High School lost the silver medal due to a penalty at the finals. It was a timing penalty that had never once occurred all season long and it blindsided me. I was shocked that we had never even received a warning in regards to the penalty. Ever. We took the bronze and moved forward. The next step became the 1989 season and a gold medal. I'm not sure if 1989 would have happened without the experience of 1988. It forced me to pay attention to details more than any previous season and it moved me to a level of clarity that I had not previously exercised.

I feel defeated when I know the performers have not had a positive experience and I certainly feel defeated when audiences are ambivalent. Loving something or hating something are both overt reactions, but complete disregard is painful. That's losing in the most personal sense of the word. That's not to say that I'm not hurt by disdain for the work we do, but hopefully I'm learning to put it into perspective. That's the thing about producing anything, competitive or not; I will constantly be confronted by new obstacles to overcome. I learn and move on and sometimes I'm a slow learner.

Losing can be fuel. And if it's a potent fuel full of discovery and excitement, it can take you far. Winning is simply another side of the same coin. Enjoy it, but know that it must be converted into a fuel of experience and confidence. I'm happy for anyone who wins and perhaps I can say that because I know the feeling. But winning and losing come with responsibility. Complacency is not an option. Both instances require what my mother had always taught me—treat others the way you want to be treated. I know I haven't had a perfect record of good behavior, but I hope I've grown from every experience and evolved. I'd love to go back in time to let the younger me know that patience really is a virtue if I can be open to the lessons at hand. There is no formula for what will be popular or what will win. It's one thing to copy other projects, but to truly find a unique voice, it's necessary to take the risk.

I'm often asked what my favorite winter color guard program is. There is not even a need for me to eliminate projects I've worked on because my favorite show is one that I had nothing to do with aside from the fact that I was an active participant in the audience. I was already a fan of Karl Lowe and the incredible performers and team at Odyssey by the time 1987 came around. In 1986 Odyssey and State Street competed to a championship tie, which I honestly enjoyed. I don't ever mind a shared title because I understand it as a circumstance that is true in the moment. It's a happenstance that actually occurred for whatever reason and accumulation of numbers. *And the more the merrier, right?* I especially enjoyed the co-champion status alongside Odyssey because I adored their style and depth of musicality, their subtlety, and the emotion they offered.

The 1987 Odyssey program was an extraordinary example of guts, innovation, and the obligation of a Champion to cover new territory. Here is a show that offered new ideas of staging, incredible vocabulary, construction, character, and an almost unbearable aesthetic of honesty all while offering a strong editorial on the existence of conformity. And the performers were invested and uniquely in sync with one another. Go and watch it sometime, because my description will never be able to do it justice.

Here is a show that proved how deeply psychological a show could become and the steps that events and motion could take in order to define the concept. All the while Odyssey worked on multiple layers, which was amazing to me. The sense of metaphor was inherently sophisticated and fantastic. It offered, and still offers, a sense of fresh perspective with each viewing. It's a show that is superbly theatrically sound and it opened my eyes to what that really, truly meant. I love it.

But guess what? This groundbreaking show not only lost the championship, it placed much lower than anyone would have expected. It was, at the time, a bit polarizing. Yet, to this day, it remains an example of going well beyond the competitive instant. The theme of the show challenged traditional notions of what a show should, or could, be. It was unlike any other presentation. Agree or disagree, the show was a winner regardless of the actual score.

There are years when I can't tell you what the competitive results were. I can't tell you who placed where or even where a group I was involved with placed. Win or lose it's ultimately about a feeling, a recollection. The years fly by and suddenly I'm left with these little gems of memories that may or may not involve winning or losing. There will always be different sides to a story, layer upon layer of perspective that simply makes it, well, life.

Successfully defining one's goals is a win/win situation. The process of making a realistic assessment harbors a different emphasis with each experience. And perhaps the ultimate pleasure of living is experiencing everything about it. The bad, the good, the win, the loss, the small step, and the big step—they all add up and soon result in a constantly changing standard of measurement. It can include winning and yet far exceed it. I've had fun winning and I've had fun losing. And sometimes, in a watercolor collage of the indescribable, I've had fun simply in the act of doing.

The opening week of the show *Odyssey* in Japan was exciting, terrifying, and overwhelming. Pulling the stage production together through technical rehearsals, rewrites, and press events was like living life in four-wheel drive. Billed as *Brass Angels* in Japan, the all female cast was showcasing their pageantry skills and finding the groove of the professional theatre routine. These first few shows were informative and I studied the audience closely. We were discovering what worked and what was falling short. We were beginning to understand the work that would fill the upcoming tour and the chance to finally have an audience was a treasure. There were notes from producers. There were poorly scribbled legal pads full of what needed to be done. I was gaining appreciation on a daily basis of what the creators and cast of *Blast!* must have been facing, and I was grateful that we were far from the London or New York critics.

After an evening performance one of our producers, Shinichi Onodera brought three Japanese women backstage to meet me. They were politely giving me their thoughts as Shinichi translated their Japanese to English for me. Their eyes filled with tears as they described their feelings after experiencing the show. They spoke of their emotional connection to the all-female cast. They described the beauty of the show and its empowering virtues. I cherished these thoughtful, beautiful women taking the time to share their thoughts with me. And in that moment they reminded me that winning could be defined far beyond numbers or awards. Exhale.

And now a story about not getting too full of yourself...

Given the vast array of definitions that winning and losing can encompass, here's a little story. In 1984, I danced for Saber and Denon Rawls in a movie starring Pia Zadora. I was young, getting a paycheck for dancing, and surrounded by the hustle and bustle of film production. I was living a tiny dream in Atlanta and didn't care if this was a B-movie or whatever. It was exciting and professional. I adored Saber and Denon and was taking in every comment, every part of the process, like the eager beaver that I was. Denon even told me that even though I didn't have the best technique that they had cast me for my communication skills and my performance at the audition. He was encouraging and even gave me positive feedback on my marching background. He liked that I could infuse the sharpness and the pop of the training. Saber and Denon had choreographed the movie *Staying Alive* among so many other professional projects and I fell into a deep admiration of their style, their professionalism, and their teaching. And FYI, Pia was extremely nice and even gave me big hug and thanked me when I informed her that I couldn't attend the cast party. I was off to the DCI convention and I did my best to explain the whole thing to her.

Now, what is this DCI thing?

After the shoot was completed I was still in Atlanta as Tam and I were planning for the upcoming drum corps season. It was winter. Tam and I were just as enthusiastic and obsessed as always. We ventured out for drinks one night in a busy Atlanta bar. We drank, we talked and talked and talked, and we were completely unaware of whomever might be around us. We were definitely lost in our own little world of winter guard, marching band, and drum corps. I think now on how much energy we had, although I'm assuming the drinks didn't hurt.

We stood at the bar when suddenly a complete stranger decided to interject himself into our conversation. Now realize, I'm pretty confident at this point. I was getting paid to do all the things I wanted to do and it was the first time I wasn't having to hold down an additional job to make ends meet. No more telemarketing, no more retail, no more temp jobs to pay the rent. I was feeling pretty good until…

> Stranger: (a bit tipsy) *What do you guys do?*
> Tam: *I teach music at a high school. I'm a music educator.*
> Stranger: *That's cool. Here in Atlanta?*
> Tam: *Yep. In the Atlanta area.*
> Tam is keeping the answers short and to the point. We both are thinking maybe he'll stumble away.
> Stranger: (quickly averting his gaze to me) *And what do YOU do?*
> Me: (taking a second to think if I could honestly say the words for the first time) *I'm a professional dancer.*
> Stranger: (looking me up and down with a hint of disgust) *Well, you don't LOOK like a professional dancer.*
> Me: (a beat) *Well, some people will tell you I don't dance like one either!*

At this point, Tam literally did the best "spit take" ever. Fortunately no one was in the range of fire. Tam put the drink down on the bar and bolted from the scene out the front door of the noisy bar. I quickly followed and found him right outside doubled over in a fit of laughter. We both howled at the thought of the moment and Tam congratulated me on one of the best comebacks he had ever heard. I think he was actually proud of me for not caving under the weight of what could have been a humiliating moment.

It just goes to show that no matter how high a wave you think you are riding, there will always be a shark underneath the surface somewhere waiting to take a bite out of your confidence.

The key is to have to find a way to laugh and it helps to have a friend at your side. Tam was the best.

There's Something to Be Said for...

CHAPTER 17

Cornbread Dressing

I cannot deny my southern roots. And every so often I catch myself being all too aware of my southernness coming out. I can still "cut" the lights on, "mash" a button and look for a "thingy-ma-jigger." As Jay reminds me I can often turn two syllables into five. The other day as I drove to the airport I spoke with my brother and sister-in-law only to hear both of them in my voice all while the conversation was actually happening. "I'll talk to y'all later. I love y'all." Sometime during my college years a group of us became aware of the southern word "Mommeranem." It's a classic used in sentences like "How's your mommeranem?" or "What's your mommeranem up to?" This is a mash-up of "mama and them" and it's said fast and smooth and flows like a friendly creek out back. It doesn't take much to put me on a southern trajectory and I enjoy it. It's comforting. And nothing is more comforting to me than one of my favorite foods, cornbread dressing.

No, dressing is not stuffing. You don't stuff the holiday turkey with dressing, but you serve it on the side and yes, the main ingredient is good ole cornbread. It's a southern favorite and just like any recipe, every cook has his or her own version. And knowing just the right touch of certain ingredients gives each and every version a unique quality. I think my mother used my grandmother's recipe when I was growing up. The ingredients along with the right amount of sage gives the house a memorable smell all full of holiday, family chatter, and good hugs. Auto-correct is trying to correct my use of the words "all full"—see? Southern. The recipe may have come straight out of the *Atlanta Journal and Constitution* for all I know. (One time I called home to ask my mother for what I thought was a very specific recipe for banana pudding. She chuckled as she told me to get the box of vanilla wafers and look on the side of the box.) I never had the wherewithal to ask my mother about the dressing before she became ill and I wish that I had. But cornbread dressing is a traditional side in my family. It always was and it is for me to this day. Once my mother was no longer doing the cooking and unable to coach my sister and my brother's wife, Carol, through the process, the recipe became a point of contention. No one ever seemed to think they were getting it right. Neither Susan nor Carol ever thought they got the recipe the way "Louise did it." I, on the other hand, could taste it just as I remembered it no matter how the ingredients were prescribed. The two of them would humorously go back and forth on the amount of milk or salt or sage or whatever. For some reason, they had enough of it right that I was instantly satisfied by the rich, memory-laden contentment of it all. Maybe the banter on getting the recipe right was part of the comfort, too. Who knows? Kitchen conversation with a good dose of love and dialect is perfection to me. A chill in the air with football on the television doesn't hurt either. The feel of a good sweater and a couple of dogs running through the house while children are laughing are also atmosphere for good, well made southern cornbread dressing. Someone should just go ahead and add those to the list of ingredients.

I think about the great cornbread dressing debates often when I think of how people long for the marching arts to stand still in time and exist just as they personally remember or experienced it. People constantly disagree on what the golden age of anything was and they always argue vehemently on the demise of the current state of well, anything. I realized a long time ago that nothing can be just as it was. Yes, it can have attributes and characteristics, it can even come close to being a perfect replica of a prior existence, but no thing can be exactly as it was before. It's just not possible. Something will always be just slightly different or not quite the same, even a Broadway revival. Now it doesn't mean that we don't try. My partner, Mark makes a great cornbread dressing and it still to this day comforts me and brings back memories that I love. Is it exactly the same? Probably not. Is it still good? Yes.

I know that my memory of those holiday feasts will always be different than the one I am experiencing and to be honest, I am now a different person, too. But we still have cornbread dressing and the holiday menu has evolved to include new dishes as well. I cherish the memory of it and I cherish what it is now in the present. It's the reason I love seeing a diverse range of shows and styles in performances. There is room for everything. History has a way of folding itself into your existence no matter how far you have traveled. I like that. The real danger would be if no one were out there still presenting traditional approaches and styles.

There is a place for every style and approach. There are all kinds of performance opportunities available for whatever the viewer or the audience might enjoy. From military tattoos to parades to football games, all kinds of styles get presented in entertaining, intelligent and informative ways. The competitive arena comes with a different pursuit. Competition challenges the realization of achievement. And certainly the more our current performers achieve the higher the standard is set. We can certainly disagree on our personal affinity for design or style choices, but to limit the competitive arena would be to bring talent, intellect and yes, entertainment to a state of stagnation. We might never discover the innovative and new, or we might not be privy to witness greatness through incredibly talented and skilled performers. If the best and brightest designers do not have a place in which to challenge limits and transcend the status quo then certainly the very activities that we all love and support run the risk of becoming a quaint relic of nostalgia. Again I would have to give my opinion serious thought if there were only one place to enjoy and practice the world of pageantry arts. But we are a world of choices and we have abundant opportunities to exercise the wide variety of styles, music, and history that continue to keep us alive and yes, healthy.

We have to remember that memory can be a fickle thing. I'm sure my recollection of so many instances is far different from the other people involved. The memory of a past era can also be better than it actually was… or not. The up side is that we actually have those memories. And I can certainly wrap my reflections in optimism given some time and distance. I think that's simply a mechanism to move forward, and I know that I have gained something from every experience.

Then there are those random things that can jump into our minds at any given moment. Here's an interesting story from 1983. It's the summer and I'm teaching with the Bayonne Bridgemen Drum Corps. We are on tour and the summer is coming to an end. Somehow about mid-summer, Sal, Tam, and I began to have discussions about my moving to Atlanta to work with the Spirit of Atlanta. I was desperate to work with Sal and Tam and this seemed like a great opportunity. That's what I remember. I don't even know if I thought it through beyond that and I made the decision as the summer tour was winding down.

I felt obligated to let The Bridgemen know my plans so they could begin to find someone to take my position. My experience there was invaluable and I appreciated it, but I knew that I had to take another step. I also didn't want them to miss an opportunity to find someone who could take them far beyond what I offered. It was difficult but I had to let the powers that be know what was happening. Here's the response I got from someone in an administrative role:

"If you don't come back here next year, I'll make sure you don't teach another DCI drum corps!"

Really? That's a pretty aggressive threat.

OK, that was 1983 and as I write it's 2015. Can you believe that memory still leaps into my mind like some sort of deranged flashback? In my head it has Darth Vader's voice. I've never regretted the decision even though I sincerely loved so many people there. It's a reminder of how important it is to really think about personal decisions and to be prepared for whatever the reaction might be. I know I did the right thing and it was right to be upfront about my decision. Once again, there are memories to remind you of a lesson learned. Move on.

There are memories that become sweeter with time. Our high school graduation ceremony was not unlike so many similar ceremonies. It was full of excitement, enthusiasm, and a wide-eyed innocent gaze into the future. The Rome City Auditorium was full of family, friends and a very real sense of community support. We sat in our crisp, satin-like Kelly green gowns with tassels dangling in our peripheral vision. We listened to speeches, received our diplomas and celebrated this ending as a brand new beginning. At the conclusion of the ceremony we made our way up the aisles to make our exit. As I made my way up the incline of the auditorium I was surprised at the sight of my brother. He stepped away from his seat to shake my hand. It was a small yet important gift of acceptance and a memory that has aged well. The smallest gesture can speak volumes. The tiniest memory can unfold into precious fuel. Move on.

"A man of great memory without learning hath a rock and a spindle and no staff to spin"
---George Herbert

FWD March

CHAPTER 18

Putting It Together (Well, for Now)

When I began writing down whatever this turns out to be, I actually thought I would spend a lot more time on my arrival at certain aspects of the creative process. But the more I ramble and purge, the more I realize that the creative process is a constantly changing idea. I can give some thoughts that mirror my current state, but I am hesitant to commit to them as "rules." Everyone must find his or her own way. You take a little here, or a little there, absorbing information and concocting a recipe that works for any given circumstance. I have absolute convictions for what I may say is designing, choreographing, or realizing a competitive pageantry program. Yet, it can all be altered at any second and hopefully, I can remain open to that. The tiniest bit of spice can suddenly change the entire recipe. *Why am I lapsing into food related references?* Here are some thoughts for here and now: an evolution of accumulated experiences, ideas, and influences that have worked for me. For me.

Music

It is essential to form a relationship with the music. In many instances the soundtrack might be incredibly experimental or it may be a classical piece redefined. The possibilities are infinite when it comes to sound, even including the absence of sound. The more you can become a student of music, the better you will be equipped to engage a partnership with it.

I am constantly seeking the advice of those who have made music their livelihood. I've learned not to be afraid to ask questions. Music is a never-ending educational process. I stand quietly by and listen to musicians talk shop. I listen to everything from a variety of musical genres to the rhythm of the subway train on a walk through the city. Years ago, I had my aura read by a psychic who told me I was surrounded by music. It's a true statement even if it could be said about anyone, anywhere. I can walk the streets of Tokyo to the sounds of J-Pop or cry to the strains of Mahler's Fifth. I smile when I hear a Scott Joplin rag and I feel certain that Betty Buckley is singing "Corner of The Sky" from *Pippin* especially for me. I am moved to this day every time the party guests sing "good-bye" to the Von Trapp Family children in *The Sound of Music*. I yearn for perfect pitch when a hummingbird whizzes by with its one-note propulsion. I stand a bit taller when I hear Madonna sing "Express Yourself." Copland's "Fanfare for the Common Man" makes me gaze upward and "Amazing Grace" reminds me of my father's mother with her ever-faithful stately elegance. I want to twist and bend to the sound of Reich or rap. I can revisit my grandparent's farm when I hear Hank or Dolly. Joni Mitchell makes me long to be more poetic and Brubeck turns me a cool blue. Bette Midler makes me want to be authentic and real while Bowie makes me want to be outrageous and rare. The list could go on and on and even if my words delude me, the emotions do not.

Our partnership with the audio fosters our ability to interpret. Whether it's literal or not, that relationship enables us to explain the unexplainable. We must nurture that relationship and learn.

Get out of Your Own Way

Getting out of your own way is one way of saying that it's not only about you. Equally as important for the performer as well as the designer, here is a statement that reflects the edict that it really is about the show. It's actually quite comforting and it's not a comment on one's personal, individual experience. Our own personal enjoyment and experience is certainly of great value, but when it comes to the work at hand, I have found it essential to give myself over to concept, character, and living in the theatrical, and yes, competitive moment.

I choreograph in character. I like thinking through the mood of a given moment, or taking on the persona or role of a given situation, and letting that freely translate into body or equipment. Hopefully, those two are merged into one. Characteristics, nuance, emotion, and dynamics are allowed to speak and emerge in those moments all the while with a sense of interpreting a musical instant. Sure, there are moves or skills that I personally enjoy or want to impose on any given situation. But if those moves and skills do not speak as the emotion, role, or character would, then they become a stumbling block for what should be an explanation of the given concept. Often, the expressive efforts behind the choreography can provide the proper, appropriate results. Freeing oneself of one's own, contemporary personality and situation to let the character and role take over opens the door to the truth of a moment. And once again, choreography should be specific to the program it inhabits. The same can be said for staging or costumes or any aspect that might aid explanation.

The concept of a show might be quite nondescript and abstract. It's still possible to give yourself over to the motivation behind a moment no matter how complex or implausible that might seem. A given moment might call for a rather loose description like "forceful" or "inquisitive." There are so many possibilities. And I'm open to those times when a concept might call for me to let my own personality be of great influence, but I like to think of that instance as one's own individualism being similar to the character or role or moment.

One's own ego, I think, brings a lot of baggage that is unnecessary motivation. Maybe it's easier for me to explain it by pointing out how easy it is to see when a writer or choreographer places work into a program that does not fit the moment, the concept, or the performers. Perhaps they simply liked the move, so they put it in the presentation. I see it often. Have you ever seen an entire group try to perform a skill that only one person could actually do? It happens. It requires a little thought (and sometimes editing), but hopefully every piece of information within a program serves a purpose.

It's also vital to understand how one's own particular life situation can influence the process. When we're troubled, challenged financially, or battling athletic directors for gym time and suddenly have to go and choreograph a phrase, it is damn near impossible. Frankly, the ability to surrender to the role or the motivation of a given moment is what helps you to get over it. What I have done often at times like this is to move on to a part that calls for me to access whatever mood I am experiencing.

Specific characters can answer a lot of questions for the writer. Would Juliet spin a saber the same way that Carmen would? Would the Jets from *West Side Story* move the same way medieval knights would move? Sometimes it's simply a manner of how the performer communicates the work at hand. Ultimately though, the goal is for each and every piece of a program to be specific to that particular presentation. If it looks like it could be in any show, with any music, or with anyone else performing it then it's probably not essential. I love seeing those groups that, minus the costumes and the music (say in the warm-up before a show), would indicate to me who, where, and what they were. It's easy to follow the trends of the moment when it comes to choreography and it often happens when designers are moving among multiple shows during the same season. There's always a "toss du jour" every season or a step that seems to have found its way into every program, regardless of it's essentiality. Everyone looking alike and doing the same work or the same choreography with only differences in music and costumes and altered count structures speaks nothing to the uniqueness that is possible in all of us. Let's use the example of a popular move that every competing group might be including in their show. Wanting to compete doesn't require copying that exact move in your own program, but it does provide the opportunity to find what your response to that skill would be. It might be a change of context or nuance or it very well could be finding a different skill that shows the same value of achievement. Respond don't replicate.

Now, I can't say that I've completely hit the one hundred percent mark when it comes to this idea but, hopefully, I'm gaining a better percentage with every attempt. It doesn't mean the same steps or moves can't exist in a multitude of shows or seasons, but the goal is to make each instance uniquely specific to a presentation. Writing in character helps define each and every millisecond in ways that broadens the scope of explaining what the show is about.

Logan is an example of utilizing what may, on the surface, seem to be the same skills from show to show. But changes in context, expressive efforts, and communication can give them an entirely different definition. Different characters in different shows can still use the same words, yet be saying something completely unique. Was the interpretation of the inhabitants of *Loganation* different from the world of *Carmen Lives*? I hope so. Were the ethereal Viking-inspired characters of *In the Cradle of Odin* different from those of the tango-inspired dancers in *The Zero Hour*? I hope so. Even though similar vocabulary might exist in all these programs, the expressive efforts, changes in approach, or altering gestures and nuance gave them fresh context that could only exist in its given circumstance. They were all speaking "color guard" and saying it completely different with each show.

The 2000 production *The Art of Noise* was really Logan being a heightened version of their youthful selves. Because the impetus of the program was a timeline of music, they were inhabiting a world that required them to showcase sides of their own personalities that could change on a dime and suddenly in one breath become an entirely new feeling. But I knew it would be a heightened version of their personalities given the theatrical situation. This would be an exaggeration of who they were within each and every moment. I could not expect them to totally understand the historical significance of each era of music, but I could certainly explore their particular perception of each style. Thus, when it came time to choreograph I was delving not only into the historical style, approach, and role, but also projecting myself into their own exuberance and awareness. It actually was fun and forced me to get to know them and constantly be aware of whom they were as young people and performers. This would be their own contemporary reinterpretation of a variety of styles and characters.

There's no denying that you are a part of it all. You are, after all, "you" in the act of creation. But the desire to make each and every moment unique to its own circumstance truly does bring forth a depth of conceptual explanation that only aids in the process and ultimately, the result.

"Why" explains "How"

Actors often search for "how" to deliver a line. When they explore "why" the character is saying the line, it can offer a brand new key to unlock the "how" the line is spoken. It's all about discovering answers. And it certainly is the means by which an actor expresses his or her intention, no matter how abstract or literal it might be.

Many times the "why" is simply to interpret the music. Musical phrases, like choreographed phrases, are contoured with expressive components (space, time, weight, flow). How the performer makes use of the expressive components can bring about numerous options for explanation. Take a phrase of equipment work or dance (or both) as an example. For you "non-spinning" folk, think of a well-known line from a movie or play (say, "To be or not to be, that is the question"). Now deliver that example solely based on the mechanics of its content. Now perform the phrase with sadness. Now perform the phrase as if you are standing before a large, scary monster. Perform the phrase as if you have just won the lottery. You can apply your own descriptions or even subdivide the phrase so that one part is interpreted one way while another is interpreted completely differently. These are all exercises in "why" and they are simplified ones for sure. The "why" can become quite emotionally complex especially when dealing with telling a story or strong narrative.

In broader terms, the concept of a presentation (the "why") directly influences "how" it is designed. Exhibiting pure musical interpretation can be the concept for a program. When established from the onset, and consistently explained throughout, it's a wonderful thing. A specific "style" is also a fun concept to observe, but again, it calls for its own unique explanation throughout the show. Clovis West High School, the marching band and the color guard, was a great example of a group that exuded a style so uniquely their own that it was worthy of taking the conceptual lead. The wonderful thing about Clovis West was that there were multiple layers to any show they presented. But both of the considerations of music and style, as any other idea, are multi-layered coded opportunities that deserve full exploration.

A few years ago after traveling for WGI to give overview commentary at regional competitions, I began to think about the "why." Guards would take to the gym floor to the announcement of their show title and then proceed to perform choreography. Their moves and phrases, even their staging seemed not to fit with their intention. They weren't doing a show about what was just announced. Sometimes, it seemed to have nothing to do with what they said they were going to do. It left the audience with an unexplained hypothesis. Sometimes it would begin one way and suddenly take a turn into something that made no sense. It would be a collection of moves that offered nothing more than being exactly that, a bunch of moves. I'm continually open to the fact that I may not be getting "it." That's one issue, of course, but we can often tell the difference. And I'm always open to more viewings in order to get the point. And the "why" can have a number of meanings for sure.

There are plenty of shows that I don't initially "get." When I see *Cirque* shows I often have an entirely different idea about the narrative and horizontal makeup of the show than what resides in the written description. It's a testament to so many great works that we can personally involve and invest ourselves into the work in a way that might be quite different from the intent. But somehow we know it works. Somehow their version of "why" is in place and we instinctively follow its trajectory. It's similar to seeing something in a painting only to find out that the artist had an intention dissimilar to our own interpretation. We still appreciate and cherish the experience. And certainly a presentation that is open to the viewer's own interpretation can be wonderful experience. The point is that there is a basis for something well formulated and detailed no matter how complex or simple it might be. And just like the imagination, the possibilities are endless.

The Simple Sentence

Sometimes we try to say too much. Too much drill. Too many notes. Too much choreography. Too much equipment work. Knowing how to be succinct, precise, and to the point is a treasure of clarity. Making the most meaningful choices to bring a thought to life is something that takes time and trust. We always want to do more. We always want to make our point over and over to feel understood. Sometimes speed is worthwhile and sometimes, so is stillness. They both take considerable control and mastery. Restraint can be a virtuous undertaking. Imagine a painter choosing just the right color for just the right point in a painting. Everything comes down to choices. Putting the thoughts together in just the right way causes a contrast and a wealth of information. And hopefully the totality of a program presents a variety of opportunities and showcases the competitor's ability to exhibit a broad, diverse range.

The *Felliniesque* ballad was a great example of brevity that, in its restraint harbored more emotion and musicality (and control) than we ever imagined. We had to choose our words wisely and the performers had to speak them clearly. It took incredible mastery and an understanding of speed from the performers. The additional concern of how all the performers had to feel the pulsation of one another is just as much an achievement as the quickest of moments.

It's a bit like poetry. The words or sounds that make up a poem could be lifted in isolation. They could very well be words or sounds that are used every day by millions and millions of people. They may have existed throughout history. There may also be words or sounds that are completely made up. But take the word or sound and surround it with any particular order of other words or sounds and the result can constantly change. It can express different ideas, feelings, and tone. It is contextual. Now the same came be said for the full sentence that has now been constructed. Is it a sentence full of big words? Is it a sentence of very small words? Is it a mix of the two? Is the sentence short or long? Is it riddled with punctuation or simply a period for its ending? Are all the words equal or is there a noun or an adjective? You get where I'm going with this lest I have to ask another question, right? The answer is in making one's point. The sentence could be complex or simple, but remember the value of both choices. Give them clarity and context.

I wish I had understood that idea when I was younger. I was constantly piling on volumes of moves and skills out of youthful eagerness. But it does remind me of how important it is to make every moment count. I've often told people that you want credit for every single action performed from as many judges as possible. And you have to remember that every single moment, no matter how secondary or unimportant you might believe it to be, gives information about your intent. What might be considered transitional is just as important as the focal point. Everything speaks and every moment carries information. The adjective is just as important as the noun is just as important as the verb is just as important as the article. The concept goes on and on.

It's to our advantage to never underestimate simplicity. We know we can see a modern painting and think, "Well, anyone could do that." The fact of the matter is anyone didn't. That artist made that distinctive idea happen. Jay tells a story about a college professor who had made that statement to a student and I think it's incredibly profound. It's so easy to look at, for example, a Rothko or Pollack and, if without any thought, say, "Well, I could do that." You better remind yourself, "I didn't!" That's not even going beyond the sheer arrogance of such a statement to actually try and execute the technique(s) involved. And we can't forget that when we think that way, we are dismissing the total originality of the work. The originality of the actual thought is astounding in its own right.

Hide the Counts

Never be afraid to move beyond the basic quarter-note beat of the audio phrase. Our marching world roots, full of tradition and historical significance, are inherently built upon the "1-2-3-4" of downbeats. There is a whole choreographic world beyond that.

Now given what is being interpreted, sure, these are important elements.

Going beyond what is the basic downbeat is an implication of rhythm. Exploring the universal opportunities of rhythms superimposed on any given audio can take the roof off creativity. Again, choices live in the options of simple versus complex. It equally applies to choreographic action.

As an observer, I appreciate my focus being on the performance and the intent at hand, which far exceed my awareness of the count structure. Unless it's absolutely your concept to only showcase structure, it's pretty fun to NOT see the counts.

Throughout the years, I have taken to simply feeling free to choreograph and improvise to the audio or music. Counts can be assigned once I've crossed the hurdle of "saying" what I want to say. Feeling the music, the character and the moment take precedence over any requirement to be fastened to a given count structure. And, guess what? It's more fun that way.

Synergize

By making the training of the body a priority, chances will bode well that there will be a harmony between the equipment and the physical requirements. The more the body is being used in so many ways in tandem with equipment, the more imperative it is that they be actively married to one another.

More and more people have begun posting short clips online. Often extremely talented and superbly creative, I notice many times exactly how they prioritize one element over the other. The equipment work can be interesting and skilled, yet the body underneath it, although active, remains disconnected and "out of sync." Often it's the lack of training. Sometimes it's a lack of thorough engagement. Training both body and equipment equally and designing with their inherent and specific harmony can bring about a wonderful result.

It's the reason I love watching great baton twirlers and rhythmic gymnasts. The separation between the body and the apparatus is invisible. One cannot exist without the other. Even in complete stillness this fact remains true. It was a Stanley Knaub lesson I have never forgotten.

For performers, it's more economical. Opposing forces can pull the energy and deter one's ability to express the intent. And remember, this idea is speaking directly to the training of the body and equipment and its achievement.

Quality over Quantity

Rehearsing and training have two very different points of view. Training gives you the muscle to speak and rehearsals let you engage in the act of a specific context. It's not unusual to hear people boasting of the hours and hours they have spent in the rehearsal process. But rehearsing and training devoid of intelligence, balance and focus is nothing more than the spinning hands of a clock. Work smart. Sometimes the endless hours are necessary and sometimes it's simply better to efficiently get the job done.

Motivate

Enthusiasm can be medicinal and invigorating. It can solve a lot of problems and carry us through the tedious hours of technical rehearsals or slow moving discovery days. Enthusiasm can console a competitive loss or turn an obstacle into a playground. Feeling motivated is not so difficult in the good times, but finding that motivation and enthusiasm in the tough times is a test.

I rely on any number of ways to get motivated from my imagination to reminding myself, sternly, that I have a job to do. I find that every day can be different. I can find motivation from imagining the audience, or catching the exuberance of the performers, or watching collaborators work. It's ever changing and I think it's the same for everyone no matter what the responsibility.

I enjoy the fantasy that I can create in my head on the not-so-easiest of days. I can imagine all kinds of scenarios where we go through our paces and create and collaborate. I remind myself that all over the world there are artists and performers working diligently in much the same way. I embrace that we are part of that world with all its fantastic possibility. It is show business. It is sport. It is unique. And often, those ambitious aspirations manifest into a reality of the task at hand being an elevated product.

Enthusiasm can't save a bad show or unfulfilled ideas, but it can sure make it better. And it can certainly make the experience survivable and present the performers as well as the audience with clarity to understand the lessons at hand. Enthusiasm, however, can propel a good program into greatness. The lack of motivation and enthusiasm however, can, for certain, pull a good show down and take everyone involved with it. So whether it is on a daily basis or in the overall scheme of things, finding motivation and accessing the electricity of enthusiasm will yes, move you forward.

Some days are just darker than others. The beauty of a team endeavor means that it's OK to be honest and it's OK to rely on fellow performers or staff members for some good energy. I like the fact that we can all have one another's backs. There is great comfort in that thought. Enthusiasm is infectious.

Ultimately we have to be professional, do our job and find our motivation. There's a reason that the old saying of keeping your eye on the prize holds true. We have to understand that before we know it we will be at the end of it all marveling at how quickly the time has passed. We will stand at the end of one road and ponder the next step.

Be Unique

You'd think this never needed to be said, right? I'll keep this short and sweet. Be cautious when it comes to trends. Even when it comes to specific moves or skills, we have to choose our words wisely. If it's appropriate for the intention then it's a viable option. If there's a way to take our own instinct and transform it into something uniquely our own, that's even better. It's also another example where context can be a key component to elevating the ordinary to the extraordinary.

Take the age-old example of several color guards in the warm-up area all dressed in black. Minus the accouterments of costume and music, would the onlooker be able to tell which guard was which? If the answer is "not necessarily" then we have a problem. I've learned that the key is to embrace what makes you and your performers special. There is and should be only one you. I love that! Even if it means following a different path, diverting ourselves from the most popular trends, and perhaps even paying a price for doing so, originality will teach us valuable lessons.

The bottom line I suppose, comes down to working together, having a feeling or idea, and putting it in front of people. Sometimes it works and sometimes it does not. Sometimes it's popular and sometimes it is not. And sometimes I just think I'm talking too much trying to make my point when in all actuality I'm just thinking out loud. Hopefully you can find through a few of my stories here and there that there is something to be discovered in whatever you have lived and experienced. Move forward. There is no formula. There is no formula. If there were a formula, someone would be very rich. And that someone would not be me, because I have not found it. *Smile*. Although I will say that I'm very glad that there is a formula for certain things like Coca-Cola. So I don't want you to think I'm completely anti-formula.

Audacious

Intrepidly daring. Bold. Marked by originality and verve. I think "audacious" is a marvel of a word. It speaks to an aspect and approach that I constantly keep in my mind. There's also a sense of rebelliousness to the concept and it challenges normal restraints. I can't speak for everyone, but

I certainly think the "audacious factor" plays an important role in standout performances and designs.

Audacity is not limited to one particular approach or style. Historically, we have seen this aspect in a multitude of shows. Bishop Kearney, Odyssey, The Cavaliers, The Blue Devils, Phantom—no matter the venue or medium, the shows that have ignited forward momentum have all carried the idea even if they did not win. Take a look back at the very first entrance of The Seattle Imperials into the competitive indoor color guard arena. It was beautiful, skilled, and still catapulted the activity into new territory. It was a moment of stunning innovation. The St. Anthony's Imperials, graceful and elegant, daring in their control and refinement, refused to be anything less than everything they were. Classic style. The electro-tilt ending of The Bluecoats, Pride of Cincinnati's *Summer of Love* using the entire performance area, the single table in Emerald Marquis's *Age of Anxiety*—the examples of memorable audacity are rich and challenging. And it goes far beyond, although can often embrace, shock value. Sometimes it's a show concept, sometimes it's a musical choice, and at other times it is simply the fearless performance of what could have been an ordinary idea. I think all great shows have had the "audacity factor" and it resonates in ways that separates a show beyond the mediocre. I find that often when there is an uncertainty of fulfillment, it could very well be the absence of audacity.

Audacity turns what could very well be just another "show" into an "event." It is an idea that runs the risk, like the tightrope walker, of falling perilously from the high wire. But it can also be a risk that takes us above and beyond our initial idea.

Take One Step

An idea can be overwhelming. The start of a new project can be overwhelming. You know the gust of wind that can seemingly arrive from nowhere and cause a cyclone of whirling motion? Even when we see the spiral of leaves or dust from a distance, we are rendered frozen in time as we watch it getting closer and closer and closer. That's the inside of my brain when it's time for something new to happen. It is the cyclone of ideas while the sound of the clock ticks away and the pages of the calendar fly. Often I feel like I absolutely and genuinely don't know what to do. It's internal chaos. And not only is it chaos, it feels like the big bang within the tiniest of spaces. And the more I experience it the more pressure I feel. If you ever have the desire to feel utterly helpless and insecure, stand in front of the most talented performers in the industry knowing that the time has come to produce something wonderful and memorable. The angst looms large and I had better not let it take up too much space. And don't even get me started on the times when the peripheral advice givers offer up those gems like, "just make it creative" or "do something really effective" (as if they couldn't see that albatross on my back already).

The entire process becomes an act of organizing all that brain activity into a singular, multilayered, hopefully well-defined thought. Focus. So how does one start? This time the answer is simple. Take just one single step. First of all, don't set up any rules. The genesis of any endeavor is license to thrill. Dream big. Let inspiration determine how to begin and it can happen in any number of ways. But just take one step. Solve one problem. Answer one question, any question. Write it all down and it can be out of order, scribbled, sketched, doodled, and abstract. Maybe there's one image that gets lodged in our head. Maybe it's a piece of music or a sound or a rhythm. Slowly, but surely we can start to organize the ideas into something that begins to make sense. No matter what, find one thing to latch on to and move forward. Answer one question, any question. Sometimes it begins to snowball and other times it might be a slow cooker. Either way is perfectly OK. As long as we're making progress it doesn't matter how fast or slow the evolution occurs. Answer one question, any question.

The jigsaw puzzle of a show begins with one unassuming piece, even if the puzzle is all sky.

Ending

It doesn't hurt to know where we are going with an idea. I wish I could say that I always knew what the ending of a project was going to be, but that's not true. I have had images of the ending, or a feeling, or sometimes it is just an infinite horizon with nothing in focus. Often I have an idea of the ending and haven't fully determined the details.

The more I write these thoughts down the more I become aware of how metaphorical they are. These modest little tidbits of suggestions can be simply about living life.

Get out of your own way and know that why you are doing something can tell you how to do that very thing. A simple sentence can be just as telling as a complex one, so know the difference in speaking volumes or remaining silent. Don't get stuck on existing solely in the quarter notes of day-to-day life and strive to let all the parts of your life find a harmony. Be uniquely you and learn to speak with your own voice understanding that sometimes we all speak in unison and other times we stand alone. Find your motivation. Begin every day with just one step by taking one action that can ignite the motion.

And now a story about standing alone…

London. Sometime mid-nineties. I had traveled for a short trip to Europe with Jeff Namian and we found ourselves watching the incredible Patti Lupone in the Terrence McNally play *Master Class*. I was mesmerized not only from the whole travel experience, but also by seeing an icon in a live performance. It was astounding to me. It's the West End and it's theatre and I am spellbound. I can be silly and sappy when it comes to those moments where I find myself present in the realization of what is happening. I can be brought to tears by the music of Stephen Sondheim or Stephan Schwartz no matter what the show or the situation. Needless to say, I found myself melodramatic in knowing exactly where I was in this precise moment. And it's Patti Lupone.

The show ends and I of course am caught up in the instant and totally forgetting that we are in (clear your throat) Great Britain. London audiences (and I knew this) don't always react in the same manner as American audiences. It's not a judgment; it's just the way it is. So here we are at the end of the show and it's time for the curtain calls. Of course there is applause…of course. Patti Lupone comes out for her bow. Applause.

Jeff and I stand for the ovation. And… we are alone. Here we are in this beautiful theatre after this beautiful performance willing to show our admiration and appreciation and we are the only two people standing. Of course it feels like time begins to slow down to a low bass hum and all eyes shift to us; those silly American boys leaping to their feet who might as well be shaking pom-poms and waving Old Glory.

At this point Jeff reacts in what is probably some sort of telepathic order from the rest of the audience. He dutifully sits back down. Not only does he sit down, he sits back down as if it never happened. This means I can feel his demeanor joining in with the collective consciousness of the audience and he's now a part of the hive mentality. *Oh well! I ain't sitt'n down, damnit! It's Patti Lupone!*

And there I stood, applauding an icon and grateful for having seen her gift in person. Now remember this is me we are talking about, me and my vivid imagination. So I am convinced that Patti Lupone absolutely recalls this one night out of her voluminous, illustrious career and will one day recognize me and show me some grand gesture of appreciation in return. I'm thinking like a T-shirt or an invitation to dinner or a phone call where she consults with me on her next project. She'll tell me her favorite Blue Devils Drum Corps show and we'll dish about how Andrew Lloyd Weber is not speaking to either one of us. We'll have drinks and swear a lot. *What? It could happen.*

So sometimes we will stand alone. We can be unapologetic and proud of the tiniest statement. Dear Patti, call me.

(A quick) EIGHTEEN AND…

After I moved to California I was asked to teach at Beyer High School with the marching band and color guard. Let me rephrase that: the band director, Gary Gilroy, hunted me down and basically would not take no for an answer. It was hilarious. Gary is not only an outstanding musical teacher, but arranges as well. He has boundless energy and is one of those rare people that exude enthusiasm to the point that gives Niagara Falls a real challenge. Enthusiastic people are priceless and when coupled with knowledge and talent, we might as well buckle up because we are in for a thrilling ride.

Gary built and maintained a high level program at Beyer and the students responded to his energy and excitement. I stayed through 1996 and spent a great deal of time developing the color guard beyond spinning flags and props. We were able to bring aboard wonderful staff and the color guard soon became competitive and continued to rise through the ranks after I had completed my time there. The color guard was an interesting case study. First of all, they had that wonderful ability to amp up the energy level during a performance that I found amazing. They didn't always rehearse with the same firework communication that could suddenly reveal itself when an audience was present. Secondly, we had to start to broaden their equipment training beyond flag and the young performers embraced the challenge whole-heartedly. Where many Scholastic programs might take the building process as a chance to compete at lower levels of competition, Beyer jumped right into the World Class competitive divisions locally and nationally. They will forever be an example of desire coupled with a program that would use every resource available to take on a challenge to work at the highest level. They didn't have all the talent or the money or the facilities that one would expect from a group with such high aspirations, but again, desire and diligence took hold.

Longing for somewhere to work a little closer to where I lived made the move to Logan an easy one. I've already written a bit about my experience with the James Logan World Guard and I still find it not only my standard for scholastic experience, but also an extraordinary time that does not come around often at all. I still can't believe the incredible performers that have come from Logan. Even after all these years, I still see that spark and inconceivable talent that emanates from Union City, CA.

I spent nine years with Logan, eight of those years being consecutive gold medal performances at WGI. I'm not bragging when I write it,

I'm just as amazed by that record as anyone and it certainly wasn't just me—there was a team mentality, a grand cohesiveness, and gifted, dazzling performers. But they were, after all, still high school students, which also adds to my amazement.

During my last year at Logan, 2005, I would be reminded in a single instant that these were still young people with lives outside of my super-focused goals for them. It was our last rehearsal before departing for Dayton, Ohio for the WGI World Championships and one of our senior members was missing. Phone calls were made, questions were asked, inquiry after inquiry until it was brought to my attention that the young man was home sleeping. I still don't know the circumstances surrounding the incident, but I do recall my screaming over the phone at his mother. It was something I had never done before and I felt awful about it. Remember I'm the person, for better or for worse, thinking the WGI Championship might as well *be* the Olympics. I fought for every ounce of quality and excellence and I wanted them to know they were as important as any performance of any kind. I wanted them to reach their potential and continue to set the standard for what a scholastic competitor could be. I was driven for sure and quite taken at this surprising episode that was so out of character for this winter guard. Well, the young man made the flight as we departed for WGI and was fine during our time in Dayton.

Once the championships were over and I could collect my thoughts I had to assess my reaction in that moment and really question if I was taking the whole thing too seriously. *Maybe.* But mostly with the completion of that championship I was feeling a need to step away and catch my breath. It could be that I was still reeling from my outburst. It was not necessarily a physical concern, but it was certainly a creative consideration. You have to know when to take some time to recharge. For me, the eighth gold medal for Logan felt like a completion of sorts. It felt like the top of Mount Everest. When you reach that kind of pinnacle what do you do? Where do you go from there? More? My primary concern was the programs we were presenting and setting the communication skills free. I wasn't sure I had another program in me and I certainly wasn't going to do just "any old" thing to win again. I'm not the manager/director type either and my creative instincts tend to go "all in." It really had become much more than winning or losing. And I loved the color guard at Logan. I still do. They are extraordinary!

My decision to move on was made. It would be time to step away and let a fresh new energy take hold at Logan. They have continued their level of excellence, creativity, and achievement and I am grateful for that. I'm lucky to have been a part of it and I'm lucky to have been a part of history.

If you can't tell it so far in this book, my mind can ricochet with thoughts that can be symptomatic of an attention issue. I own it. I've known it for a while now. I constantly have to slow down, take a breath, and focus. So my journey to teach in Japan had begun in the mid-nineties and now the opportunities there were increasing. Wayne Downey had enlisted my help there in what would become a long list of established collaborators. Working with the SOKA Renaissance Vanguard as well as other fine groups in Japan has been a new perspective and a much appreciated creative challenge. My departure from Logan allowed for different experiences and I'm fortunate to still create drill, staging, and costumes for them during the marching band season. Was I totally getting rested and a much needed vacation from my own obsessive impulses? Nope, not at all. However, I was certainly reconfiguring the way I spent my creative time, which included collaborating more. I think that has been important.

I'm writing this on an express train from Tokyo to Narita. It's January and hopefully now things will slow down a bit. I hope I'm learning when I need to press pause and catch my breath. I'm not a workaholic like I think some people are, but I do feel constantly caught in a barrage of creative necessity. There's still work to do, shows to plan, ideas to birth, and though I have no vacation plans, it's time to recharge. Wish me luck. I really don't want to feel the way my driver's license photo looks.

Putting It Together (Well, for Now)

CHAPTER 19

Dear Performers...

Dear Performers, there is no one like you and we are nothing without you. Whether you are a musician, a dancer, color guard member, or a twirler, you have provided enjoyment, entertainment, and emotional experiences to more people than you will ever know. You represent a history of people who have come before you and felt the common bond that showcases talent and skills. And you are part of a continuum that will extend into the days, years, decades, and centuries ahead. You are a part of something bigger than you can imagine. It reaches from the past to the very spot you stand today and is planting the seeds of imagination in young minds that will bring forth the future.

There was no reasonable explanation for how the idea of all this reached out to me. Maybe it was some fleeting glimpse of a majorette that caused me to detach the cardboard cylinder from a coat hanger and begin to twirl. No one in my family was involved in marching band, twirling, or their extensions. My father had a momentary venture of playing a bugle in his scout troop, but it wasn't something that would have been conveyed to me at the age of four or five. There was certainly music in the house. All kinds of music came alive in our home. There was classical music from the television or country music on the radio or the sound of Elvis and the Beatles coming from my sister's room. My brother listened to Hendrix or the Allman Brothers. My father would sing church hymns, Sinatra or Hank Williams. We were at church at least three times a week if not more, and the sound of the church choir and the richness of the church organ and baby grand piano were imprinted on me from the start. The organist sat me on her lap and held my small hand in order to move my fingers across the keyboard. With her assistance, I was tracing the melody of "Onward, Christian Soldiers" and the sound resonated from speakers throughout the sanctuary. I have no idea how I remember that, but I remember my amazement of it all. The sound of the high school marching band drifted to our neighborhood and I could hear it from inside and outside the house. And this was old-school marching band with its fuzzy busby hats and high leg lifts and glittery, sequined majorettes. I was surrounded. It was a natural state of being for me no matter what variety of music pervaded my tiny world.

Eventually (and I was still only about four or five), I was taken across the street to watch the high school band practice. I was allowed to march beside the tallest of tall drum majors and mimic his high leg lift and triumphant attitude. I intently made the effort to match his sizeable strides from yard line to yard line. I saluted and conducted and signaled commands with my imaginary whistle. I was aware of rhythm and I was aware of how it was entertaining the onlookers. It's an alarmingly vivid memory. Somewhere in there, unbeknownst to me, a path must have been set.

Performers, in ways large and small, you are making an impression. And the importance of your impact is the same either way. In the great family of us all, you are the ones moving us forward. And it doesn't even matter if you are aware of it or not, it is happening by your sheer dedication to the exchange of emotion and communication. You are sharing something as big as humanity. You are living the arts. Music and motion like the hum of the earth's vibration in a constant spin. You are part of something worthy and transcendent.

Take that knowledge with you as you find your own unique way. As you train, interact with others and experience the joy of live performance, rest assured that no one can take away the past, the present, and the future of what you are doing. Be grateful for the smallest lessons as well as the big lessons. It makes no difference if someone doesn't understand what you are doing. You understand it and you carry with you the knowledge that those before you and those yet to come have and will understand it also. And the answers you discover will be revealed in numerous ways. We are part of a universal rhythm and the global pulse marches onward. You know how to sense the interval of those on either side of you and can jettison your individuality into the spotlight at just the right moment. We can collectively put heel to ground at the heart of a downbeat and we can make eye contact with a bystander or a fellow performer.

When I was in elementary school I would collect some clothing and place them into one of my brother's gym bags. I made my way to the steps leading from our den out into the back yard. I would assume a regulatory sitting position on the concrete steps diligently waiting for an imaginary bus to arrive. After an allotted amount of time, the fantasy of a bus would arrive and I would get on board making my way out into the big backyard. In my mind I could make the hour-long trip in a matter of steps and I was determined and confident as I disembarked from the bus onto the waiting grassy area. In my fantasy I was going to band camp. I would place the emblazoned gym bag to the side and proceed through the paces of practice. Now I have no earthly idea how I even knew what band camp was or is. Band camp, that time when many marching bands take off to different campgrounds or college campuses to learn and practice the upcoming seasonal show, is a regular part of the schedule for many high school programs. But at that time it certainly wasn't on the schedule for our local high school and they usually spent what amounted to band camp on the school grounds a few weeks before classes would begin. Yet I played the scenario out in my head turning it into a tiny reality with fervor and determination. I would practice marching basics, I would act as the drum major and I would move back and forth, back and forth across the imaginary football field. I acted the whole thing out all while humming music or clicking sticks together. I have no idea how I could even come up with this entire idea, but I remember clearly playing it out quite seriously. I scheduled the time and I heard the corrections and took orders in my head. It was all quite bizarre, but I think a bit awesome, too. *How did I know this?* But somehow I think it was in the air and somehow I caught that fleeting molecule of an idea and made it playtime. I wonder what neighbors must have thought of me parading in a make-believe drill around the backyard. How peculiar it must have been to see this little guy marching away the hours for no apparent reason. It's funny and sweet and maybe some sort of strange example of how something in the universe reaches into the smallest of imaginations.

You see, this thing you do, full of music and motion, enthusiasm and commitment is released into the atmosphere. And somewhere that giddy, bony boy on fresh cut Georgia grass is capturing that rat-a-tat-tat street beat and turning it into a dream. I have no explanation and somewhere along the line I have decided that I don't need one.

Dear performers, from whatever level you are active, from whatever time in history you exist, no matter what the style, or music, or movement, I am grateful. You have started families and embarked on your own life adventures. Many of you have pursued artistic careers and have achieved a staggering amount of wonderful success. You are journalists, academics, designers, filmmakers, comedians, musicians, teachers, nurses, and the list goes on and on. We've made one another laugh and made one another angry. We've been right and we've been wrong. But it is an honor to be an observer of who you were, who you are, and who you will become.

FWD March

CHAPTER 20

Pull It in

This is what happens at the end of a rehearsal or after a performance. Every one gathers together for announcements, comments, corrections, or a general wrap-up that will bring a sense of conclusion to the proceedings. Pull it in. It's a way to unify the thoughts or remind everyone why we are where we are. It is sweaty, stinky, hungry, tired people who need to know what the schedule is and how to move forward.

So here I am trying to bring some sort of conclusion to everything I've offered so far. I'd like to think I'm going to be the badass rapper with the perfect last line followed by dropping the microphone. *Thump!* But to be honest, even from the start I have never had an ending for this book.

And perhaps I'm uncomfortable with thinking that there might actually be an ending. If you haven't figured it out by now, I am a fan of forward motion. In the great scheme of things, we really don't have a choice do we? The world will keep spinning and we will make our way through time no matter how hard we might fight it. Some things have not changed. We still live in a world where, even though progress can be made, prejudice, ignorance, and basic human rights, can be ignored. There are still those people who will persecute and commit violent acts upon fellow human beings. Sermons become social and political weapons for those who choose to demand the conformity of everyone to one religious doctrine. Racism still exists. Still. Bullying persists. Still. Harassment continues. Still. And yet, somehow survival is just as possible as it has always been. We can never surrender ourselves to some sort of acceptance of injustice or regard it as "just the way it is." But rest assured, amid your greatest challenges, you are not alone.

I've worked a variety of odd jobs from retail to restaurants. I've typed invoices and built animal cages. I've worked an assembly line checking animal pharmaceuticals. I've been so poor I was eating scraps off the plates at Ponderosa Steak House before I ran them through the dishwasher. I've mopped the sticky sediment of Junior Mints and popcorn from a movie theater floor. I spent endless hours making phone calls for a New York Telemarketing firm counting the minutes till I could take a train to go to class or rehearsal. I've pulled weeds, answered phones, and sorted mail. However…

Music and marching have brought me to this brief pause in my own forward motion. It is a powerful and awesome act of artistry that all of us, past, present, and future, are living. It is alive and it is very much an act of importance. Music and percussion and marching and dancing and color and spectacle and expression are not leaving us any time soon. It is here for the long human haul. It is a language that so very many of us understand. We comprehend it with our heads and our hearts and the pulsation of the blood in our veins. And somehow, even when there is no rhyme or reason or logic, we seem to find one another.

I don't want to come to a "halt" or make an "about face." For those of you who aren't familiar with the terms, those are commands a drum major might give.

"Mark time hut."

"To the rear…march."

"Left face."

"Right face."

"Ready…halt."

My favorite is simply this: "Ready…move!"

About the Author

George "Scott" Chandler is a member of the Winter Guard International Hall of Fame and was inducted into the Drum Corps International Hall of Fame in 2004. He has designed, choreographed, instructed and coached numerous award winning competitive groups around the world. His unprecedented competitive record includes twenty-two consecutive years of World Class champions for Winter Guard International. He is the program coordinator and choreographer for the award winning Blue Devils Drum and Bugle Corps of Concord, California and the SOKA Renaissance Vanguard of Tokyo, Japan.

A partial list of wonderful memories:
Skylarks 1982-1984
Bridgemen Drum and Bugle Corps 1982-1983
Tate High School 1986-1989
State Street Review 1984-1989
Spirit of Atlanta Drum and Bugle Corps 1984-1988
San Jose Raiders 1990-1994
Beyer High School 1990-1996
Blue Devils World Guard 1995-1998
James Logan High School 1997-2005
Blue Devils Drum and Bugle Corps 1990-present
SOKA Renaissance Vanguard 1996-present

Additional Choreography: Schaumburg Guardsmen Drum and Bugle Corps, Cadets Of Bergan County Drum and Bugle Corps, Phantom Regiment Drum and Bugle Corps, Phantom Regiment Winter Guard, St. Ann's World Guard, Full Circle Winter Guard, Blessed Sacrament World Guard, Bishop Kearney World Guard, Fantasia World Guard, Northern Lights World Guard, Syndication Twirling Team USA

Author's Notes

Who on earth does he think he is? Why would he be so presumptuous to think that anyone, anywhere would care to know anything whatsoever about him? Why now?

It's easy to hear the cynics raving with a barrage of questions before you even start. We live in an air of pessimistic voyeurism. People, amid a search for validity, waiting anxiously to simply observe from the outside, then criticize those on the inside of a very personalized journey.

We can't often agree on a definition for our world of motion and music and we certainly can't agree on its relevance. But those of us involved can all agree that it has shaped us, educated us, nurtured us, and propelled us through our lives. I think it's time to write about it more, explore it more, share it whenever possible in any form possible.

I like to think I am writing for that young Georgia boy who scoured the school library in search for a definition of anything related to marching bands, pageantry, music, and motion. I wanted desperately to read someone's story of enthusiasm and process. I needed to know that I was not alone and there was nothing I could find to define or explain what it was, or why I might be so drawn to this "thing" that I could not even describe. The library, full of analysis and exposé on a universe of subject matter, held nothing I could find, at least not at my school. I don't consider myself academically clever enough to write a history of the pageantry arts; many have long since done so. But I can tell *my* story. Everyone can tell his or her own story. And everyone should. Everyone can write his or her own book, right?

Well, you better put the disclaimer out there early. So I'm sorry to those who find my reflections obnoxious, absorbed, and much too full of hot air. I'm sorry if I offend or forget or inadvertently fall short of the complete story. I can't tell every story, mention every name, or expound on every experience. I offer my apology for the ricochet of flashbacks and time travel. This is not a history of pageantry. I simply want to put some thoughts out into this overly verbalized, cyber-glorified, hypercritical, magical universe that are sincerely my own.

And most of all, I have an impossible desire to give that small town southern boy, that comical, humorous, beaten-down, teased, bullied, talented, optimistic boy, a sense of imagination and the ability to dream, create, and understand that a hobby can become a life. No matter what anyone says. I sincerely appreciate all of you who are interested in the marching arts, or participate in music and motion and I encourage everyone to continue to tell its amazing stories and share the experience.

Glossary

Pageantry Arts: Not to be confused with beauty pageants, this is simply an umbrella term that can encompass all the activities that include marching and motion-based spectacle.

Marching Band: Including percussion, woodwind, and brass instruments, marching bands exist at many levels from elementary to high school to university. Around the world there are often independently based marching bands not associated with educational institutions. Marching bands often include color guards, drill or dance teams, and baton twirlers. They perform at celebrations, sporting events, parades, or competitions.

The Band Director: This person is the music educator.

Drum and Bugle Corps: These groups utilize brass and percussion instrumentation. They began as community-associated units such as churches or local VFW-type organizations.

Color Guard: Flags, rifles, sabers, or any variety of props are elements used by the color guard or auxiliary to interpret the music, character, or theme of the show.

Winter Guard: Color guard that competes in an indoor setting such as a gymnasium or arena to pre-recorded or live music. They use expanded set designs, costuming, themes, concepts, and sometimes lighting. Moving away from Drum Corps International's summer contest for indoor color guards, the winter season became the primary time for indoor competition and the title has often remained even though contest can occur well into the Spring.

Percussion: Percussion can actually be a two-part explanation. The battery consists of snare drums, multi-mounted drums such as tenor or quad drums, bass drums, and sometimes a cymbal line. The front ensemble or "pit" performs with a variety of mallet keyboards and specialty percussion instruments and has evolved to often include electronic keyboards.

Indoor Percussion: These percussion ensembles compete in gymnasiums or arena settings with elaborate concepts, themes, costumes, and set design.

Baton Twirling: Ranging from performance with marching bands to several prestigious world championships, the art of twirling baton is an amazing presentation of dance, gymnastics, ambidexterity, and twirling skills. Their programs have also evolved into conceptual, thematic, athletic, and intricately designed productions.

BOA: Bands of America—an organization that provides premier competitive events throughout the United States for high school marching and concert bands. Their calendar culminates in a grand national championship showcasing some of the most progressive and creative scholastic marching bands from all over the country.

http://www.musicforall.org/

WGI: Winter Guard International is the leading governing body for indoor color guard and percussion competition. www.wgi.org

DCI: Drum Corps International is the governing body for drum and bugle corps competition. The organization is primarily based in the United States although it does include some international competitors.

www.dci.org

DCA: Drum Corps Associates is the governing body for all-age drum corps or senior corps competition. They include performers without age regulations. www.Dcacorps.org

The Director: Sometimes the executive director, this is the person who makes the non-profit existence work.

The Drill Writer: The person who stages the performance. Sometimes it's geometric drill formation; sometimes it's more theatrical staging. This person really holds the key to where the performers are placed and the motion they create.

Staging: This is another word for "where" and "how" the performers are placed. The drill writer or person staging the program may be a separate person or it may also be the choreographer.

The Instructor: Instructors teach the performers and train them in technique, expression, and communication. Many times each section will have a specialist to work with them. The sabers may have a saber instructor or the flags may have a flag instructor, etc.

The Choreographer: This is the person who puts the steps or counts of work together to organize them into complete phrases and thoughts. Sometimes the person who choreographs equipment work is called the "writer." I actually acknowledge it all as choreography. Many groups have several people who take on the creative choreographic task while in other instances, like mine; it's handled by one person alone.

The Composer: This is that wonderfully genius musician who exercises his or her talent to create something unique and original.

The Arranger: This person arranges the music. This person may alter the original musical composition to accommodate the goals of a particular program. Arrangers work in brass, woodwinds, vocals, or percussion and beyond. The arranger literally "arranges" the parts of the musical audio and organizes the parts of the music choices to create a complete soundtrack.

The Orchestrator: The person who actually translates the music into the language of the specific instruments being used. Sometimes the arranger and the orchestrator might be the same person, but they are definitely two very different jobs that require great skill and talent.

The Technical Staff: These are the people who "clean" or "perfect" the choreography or musical presentation. Often these people are instructors who take on the training and follow it up with the cleaning process.

The Artistic Director: Sometimes this is a team of people or a single person responsible for the artistic direction of a program, presentation, or organization.

The Program Coordinator: This is the person who brings the efforts of the creative process together into a whole. The Program coordinator oversees every aspect of the presentation from costumes to choreography or music to staging and the pacing of the program; the complete package falls to this person.

The Music Coordinator: This is the person responsible for every aspect of the musical presentation.

The Visual Coordinator: This person is responsible for all the visual aspects of the program.

Made in the USA
Charleston, SC
10 June 2015